REDHOT
SEX

REDHOT SEX

Flic Everett

Illustrated by Alan Adler

MQP

Contents

1 FEELING **SEXY**

You don't have to look like a supermodel and be an expert on the Kama Sutra to have great, red hot sex. With a little bit of preparation – from lighting a few candles to a full-monty striptease – and lots of fun practice, you can learn how to feel like a sex god or goddess.

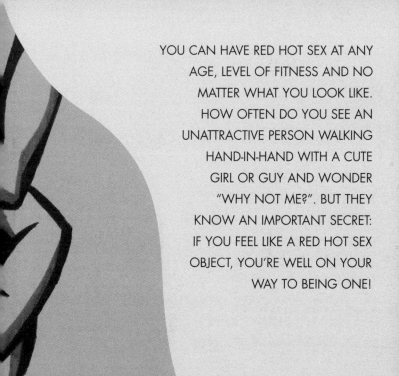

YOU CAN HAVE RED HOT SEX AT ANY AGE, LEVEL OF FITNESS AND NO MATTER WHAT YOU LOOK LIKE. HOW OFTEN DO YOU SEE AN UNATTRACTIVE PERSON WALKING HAND-IN-HAND WITH A CUTE GIRL OR GUY AND WONDER "WHY NOT ME?". BUT THEY KNOW AN IMPORTANT SECRET: IF YOU FEEL LIKE A RED HOT SEX OBJECT, YOU'RE WELL ON YOUR WAY TO BEING ONE!

Be prepared. Take a bath in scented water after a long day at the office. Choose a stimulating aroma for your bath, such as ylang ylang or sandalwood oils, to enhance sensuality. Relax, take your time and think about what you're going to get up to when you emerge from the bath. The combination of fragrant oil and warm water will make your body glow with sensuality.

ESSENTIAL OILS WITH
APHRODISIAC QUALITIES INCLUDE:
BLACK PEPPER, CARDAMOM, CLARY SAGE,
JASMINE, JUNIPER, ORANGE BLOSSOM,
PATCHOULI, ROSE, SANDALWOOD
AND YLANG YLANG

For erotic relaxation, massage your partner with body lotion or aromatherapy oils. The relaxing touch, the firm and fluid kneading of flesh and pressing of fingers on skin, is an amazing and sexy way to relax. But remember, don't get carried away – you're just working your way up to the good bit!

FOR AN ADDED SENSATION, KEEP THE OIL IN THE FRIDGE OVERNIGHT, BEFORE YOU USE IT. WHEN IT'S RUBBED ONTO YOUR SKIN, THE SUDDEN CHILL WILL MAKE YOUR SENSES TINGLE INSTANTLY, PROVIDING YOU WITH A THRILLING PHYSICAL SENSATION – AND YOU'VE NOT EVEN KISSED YET!

Peel off your lover's shirt and lay them on the bed. Slowly, start to massage their torso to relax them. Insist they remain passive while you remove their lower garments. Massage the lower body and watch those muscles start to ease. Later, be a bit more brazen and slide your hand between their legs, over their breasts, very slowly, massaging the sensitive zones.

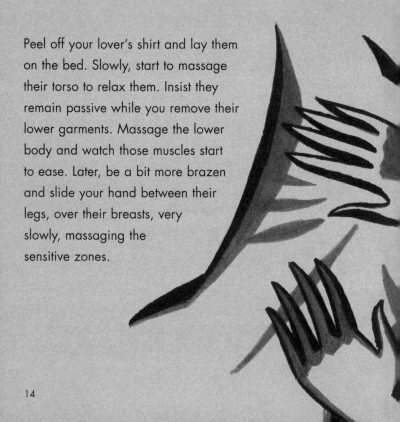

Don't rush and, if your partner's not aroused yet (this seems pretty unlikely), just continue the regular massage, keeping them warm. However, your partner is probably completely hot, but you don't want to spoil it for them by making them do any work, so indulge in a little oral sex or find a position for penetration in which you are the one who does all the work. Unfair? Just wait until it's your turn!

CHOOSE A CARRIER BASE OIL, SUCH AS ALMOND,
WITH A FEW DROPS OF ESSENTIAL OIL MIXED IN.
SENSUAL OILS INCLUDE BERGAMOT,
ROSE, SANDALWOOD AND YLANG YLANG.
(MAKE SURE YOUR PARTNER LIKES THE SMELL FIRST!)

You could use a scented lotion to massage your partner, although it will be absorbed more quickly. Natural cosmetics companies often produce sensual massage blocks, which are solid and impregnated with oil.

Cover yourselves in oil and take turns to massage – start at each other's feet, sliding right up the body, writhing gently.

TOP 10 MASSAGE TIPS

1 MAKE SURE THAT YOUR PARTNER IS WARM AND COMFORTABLE, WITH TOWELS COVERING PARTS OF THEIR BODY THAT YOU'RE NOT MASSAGING.

2 NEVER PRESS TOO HARD – REMEMBER, YOU'RE NOT A PROFESSIONAL AND YOU DON'T WANT TO PUT YOUR PARTNER'S BACK OUT.

3 USING YOUR FLAT PALMS, MAKE GENTLE CIRCLES ALONG BOTH SIDES OF THEIR SPINE.

4 USE YOUR FINGERTIPS TO MAKE SMALLER CIRCLES ALL OVER THEIR BACK, MOVING UPWARDS RATHER THAN DOWN, TOWARDS THE HEART.

5 IF YOU FEEL KNOTS OF TENSION, GO EASY – IF YOUR RUBBING HURTS YOUR PARTNER, STOP.

6 YOU CAN USE YOUR NAILS TO SCRATCH DELICATE PATTERNS ON YOUR PARTNER'S BACK.

7 YOU CAN MASSAGE THE ARMS, BY KNEADING GENTLY FROM THE SHOULDERS DOWN, WITH FIRM, LIGHTLY SQUEEZING MOVEMENTS.

8 IN A SENSUAL MASSAGE, THE BUM IS IMPORTANT – KNEAD THEIR BUTTOCKS AND WORK INWARDS AS FAR AS YOU, OR THEY, ARE COMFORTABLE WITH.

9 SOME PEOPLE LIKE HAVING THEIR FEET MASSAGED, OTHERS HATE IT. IF YOUR PARTNER LIKES IT, BE FIRM TO AVOID TICKLING – THE CENTRE OF THE SOLE IS VERY SENSITIVE, AND RESPONDS WELL TO RUBBING IN CIRCLES.

10 AFTERWARDS, COVER YOUR PARTNER – IF RELAXED MUSCLES GET COLD, IT CAN LEAD TO STIFFNESS.

Sex needn't take place only in bed. If you're
having a spontaneous moment on the
sofa, why not just stay there, or
throw some cushions on the floor
and continue. Or both. What
about some passion on the
kitchen floor? You might even
be able to reach over to the
refrigerator and grab the
whipped cream. If you have a
roaring log fire, why not slip
into your sexiest clothes and
settle down to a night on the
hearthrug.

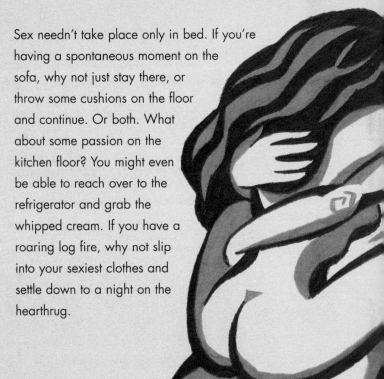

GO TO BED NAKED TO ENJOY THE FEELING OF SKIN ON SKIN, OR CHOOSE SOMETHING SILKY OR SATINY THAT WILL FEEL LUXURIOUS AND SENSUAL ON YOUR SKIN – IT'LL IMPROVE YOUR LOVE LIFE MORE THAN YOU MIGHT IMAGINE.

The more of an effort you make to feel sexy, the more you WILL feel sexy – and more confident with the exotic you. So dress in clothes that make you feel good during the day, too. Ladies, choose tactile fabrics, low-cut tops and your favourite perfume. Men, get wearing that spicy aftershave, a well-cut suit and pay meticulous attention to your grooming.

SEDUCE YOUR PARTNER. THERE'S NOTHING BETTER THAN BEING UNDRESSED BY SOMEONE YOU LUST AFTER. UNBUTTON CLOTHES, UNFASTEN BELTS AND UNCLIP BRAS SLOWLY AND LOVINGLY, KISSING, NIBBLING AND LICKING THE NEW-FOUND FLESH AS YOU GO.

TOP 10 WHAT WOMEN LIKE TO SEE YOU DRESSED IN

1 EVERY WOMAN LOVES A MAN IN A TUX – IT HAS THE POWER TO MAKE THE DUMPIEST MAN LOOK TALL, IMPOSING AND SEXY.

2 WHITE BOXERS OR BUM-HUGGING CALVINS – BUT NOT WITH A ROLL OF FLAB HANGING OVER THE ELASTIC.

3 CHUNKY JUMPER – CUTE, VULNERABLE YET SEXY, BUT NOT WITH CORDS, YOU'LL LOOK LIKE A GEOGRAPHY TEACHER.

4 WELL-CUT SUIT – SLIMMING AND TONING ANY FIGURE, A GOOD SUIT CAN GIVE SEX APPEAL TO THE LEAST LIKELY CANDIDATE.

5 NOTHING AT ALL – FOR OBVIOUS REASONS! AND OFTEN BETTER THAN ANY KIND OF POSING POUCH.

6 WHITE T-SHIRT AND LEVIS – FOR THE REBEL WITHOUT A CAUSE LOOK. IT STILL TURNS WOMEN ON 50 YEARS LATER.

7 UNIFORMS – POLICEMAN, FIREMAN, DOCTOR, OR SOLDIER. FIND OUT WHAT HER FANTASY OF A CAPABLE MACHO MAN IS, AND HIRE THE OUTFIT.

8 SILK DRESSING GOWNS – A LITTLE NOEL COWARD, BUT IF YOU CHOOSE A JAPANESE ONE, YOU CAN LOOK RELAXED AND SEXY.

9 MOTORBIKE GEAR – GREASE, ENGINES AT FULL THROTTLE OR WILD-EYED LONERS ON THE EDGE – YES, IT'S SEXY.

10 LEATHER COATS – THINK KEANU REEVES IN THE MATRIX, THERE'S SOMETHING VERY DECADENT YET MASCULINE ABOUT THE LEATHER COAT.

TELL YOUR PARTNER THAT YOU HAVE
SOMETHING SPECIAL PLANNED FOR THEM.
ORGANISE YOUR HOUSE TO GIVE IT
A SENSUAL FEEL – PLAY MUSIC, LIGHT
CANDLES (IT'S ALL VERY 70S, BUT IT
WORKS!). BANISH ANY WORRIES
ABOUT MISSING THE LAST EPISODE
OF YOUR FAVOURITE TV PRO-
GRAMME BY SETTING THE VIDEO
IN ADVANCE. YOU CAN KEEP
YOUR MIND CONCENTRATED ON
THE MORE IMPORTANT THINGS
WHILE THE VIDEO WHIRRS AWAY.

TOP 10 RELAXATION TIPS

1 RUN YOUR PARTNER A BATH. USE A WELL-LATHERED SPONGE TO 'WASH' THEM SLOWLY, POURING WATER OVER THEIR SHOULDERS, DOWN THEIR ARMS OR DOWN THEIR BACK.

2 SHARE A GLASS OR TWO OF WINE – JUST ENOUGH TO CHILL OUT, BUT NOT ENOUGH TO GET DRUNK.

3 PRACTICE YOGA, TAI CHI OR ANOTHER MEDITATIVE EXERCISE. IT RELAXES YOU AND HELPS YOU TO FEEL REFRESHED AND RE-ENERGISED.

4 GIVE EACH OTHER A GENTLE SHOULDER-RUB – NOTHING TOO HARSH, JUST SLOW, RELAXED MOVEMENTS.

5 MAKE SURE THAT THE ROOM YOU ARE IN (OR WILL BE IN) IS TIDY. THIS ONLY TAKES A BIT OF PLANNING BUT IT WILL MAKE YOU MORE RELAXED AND READY FOR LOVE.

6 LIGHT SOME AROMATHERAPY CANDLES OR INCENSE STICKS. MUSK IS FAMOUS FOR IT'S SENSUAL, EROTIC AND INTENSE FRAGRANCE.

7 INVEST IN AN INDOOR FOUNTAIN – THE SOUND OF WATER IS DEEPLY RELAXING.

8 WRITE A LIST OF EVERYTHING THAT YOU HAVE TO DO THE FOLLOWING DAY. YOU CAN THEN RELAX FULLY AND ENJOY TIME WITH YOUR PARTNER WITHOUT BEING DISTRACTED BY CHORES.

9 COOKING A MEAL CAN BE VERY RELAXING. CHOOSE A LIGHT SUPPER (SO THAT YOU'RE NOT TOO BLOATED TO MOVE AFTERWARDS) AND CHECK OUT SOME APHRODISIAC RECIPES ON THE INTERNET.

10 LEARN TO GIVE YOUR PARTNER A FOOT MASSAGE. OR SCALP MASSAGE. THESE CAN BE VERY SENSUAL AND INTIMATE. THERE ARE MANY 'TEACH YOURSELF' BOOKS IN THE SHOPS.

Ladies, go out in your normal evening wear, but forget the knickers. Then when you're standing at the bar, take his hand and place it on your bum – and from there, it's only a short persuasive step to bundling him into a toilet cubicle.

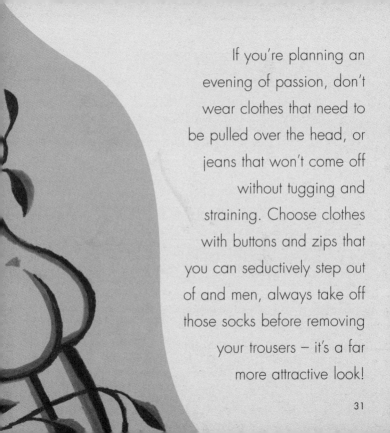

If you're planning an evening of passion, don't wear clothes that need to be pulled over the head, or jeans that won't come off without tugging and straining. Choose clothes with buttons and zips that you can seductively step out of and men, always take off those socks before removing your trousers – it's a far more attractive look!

Wait until you're in a crowded bar and are both relaxed. Slip your hand onto the crotch of his trousers and rub gently as you stand behind him. And if he gets really worked up, retreat to a dark corner, pull a coat over his lap and thrust your hand right in there. Squeeze gently, don't rub violently and be discreet!

TOP 10 GIRLS: HOW TO DO A GREAT STRIPTEASE!

1 CHOOSE MUSIC WITH A SLOW BUT SEDUCTIVE BEAT.

2 ALWAYS REMEMBER THE 'TEASE' BIT – COME CLOSE TO YOUR PARTNER, BUT DON'T LET HIM TOUCH. KISS HIM BUT DON'T GIVE HIM ANYTHING MORE THAN THAT.

3 WEAR CLOTHES WITH ZIPS, SUCH AS A FRONT-FASTENING TOP AND A MINI SKIRT. ALWAYS WEAR STOCKINGS, SUSPENDERS AND HIGH(ISH) HEELS.

4 BEGIN TO DANCE, TAKING YOUR TOP OFF FIRST. UNDO THE ZIP, TURN AWAY AND SHRUG IT OFF AND TURN ROUND WITH YOUR HANDS COVERING YOUR BREASTS.

5 UNZIP YOUR SKIRT, TURN AROUND, BEND FORWARD (MEN LOVE TO SEE A GIRL'S BUM) AND DROP THE SKIRT TO THE FLOOR, KICKING IT ASIDE.

6 CARESS YOURSELF, UNHOOK YOUR BRA, THEN TURN ROUND AGAIN AND REMOVE IT WITH A FLOURISH. TURN BACK WITH YOUR HANDS OVER YOUR BREASTS.

7 AS YOU START TO UNTIE EACH SUSPENDER BELT WITH ONE HAND, YOU'LL HAVE TO EXPOSE ONE BREAST. TAKE OFF YOUR SUSPENDER BELT AND PEEL OFF YOUR STOCKINGS, KICKING OFF YOUR SHOES AS YOU GO.

8 HOOK BOTH HANDS THROUGH YOUR KNICKER ELASTIC, PULL YOUR KNICKERS DOWN A LITTLE WAY THEN, TEASINGLY, PULL THEM BACK UP (YOU MIGHT START THIS BEFORE REMOVING YOUR SUSPENDER BELT TOO).

9 PUSH THEM TO THE FLOOR, STEP OUT OF THEM, AND YOU'RE DONE!

10 WHATEVER YOU'RE WEARING, REMEMBER, UNDRESS SLOWLY, TEASE LOTS, SHOW BITS OF FLESH AND HIDE THEM. DON'T LET HIM TOUCH YOU (THOUGH YOU CAN TOUCH HIM).

Lingerie

Dressing for the boudoir is vital, as it sets exactly the right mood and signifies that sex is on the agenda. Girls, get that sexy underwear out of the bottom drawer. Take your man's breath away by wearing his favourite lacy undies and stockings and draping yourself over the bed, over him, or even over the dinner table!

Go shopping with your partner to buy sexy underwear. Let your partner choose what he'd like to see you in and you will be certain to feel stunning (don't be afraid to experiment but don't wear anything that you won't feel at ease in.) Then it's his turn to take you shopping...

MEN LOVE WOMEN IN STOCKINGS – ANOTHER CLICHÉ, BUT IT'S TRUE. IT'S THE BARE LEG AT THE TOP THAT DRIVES MEN WILD. YOUR PARTNER MIGHT CONSIDER NOT WEARING KNICKERS UNDER A SKIRT QUITE NAUGHTY, BUT WEARING STOCKINGS WITH NO KNICKERS UNDER YOUR SKIRT WILL MAKE HIM FEEL LIKE THE LUCKIEST MAN ALIVE.

You can buy special sex lingerie, such as peephole bras and crotchless knickers. If it works for you, don't be shy – men are hardly going to laugh when confronted by it, they'll more likely be speechless. However if you prefer a subtler look, you can't go wrong with matching black or red or pink lace undies, bra and suspender belt.

TOP 10 MEN: YOU CAN STRIPTEASE TOO!

1 WEAR A JACKET, TROUSERS AND A SHIRT, WITH BUTTONS, AND GO BAREFOOT (MEN'S SHOES AND SOCKS ARE HILARIOUSLY UNSEXY.)

2 CHOOSE SOME MUSIC, BUT DON'T MAKE IT TOO MACHO BECAUSE YOU'LL NEVER LIVE UP TO THE IMAGE!

3 DON'T FORGET TO TEASE YOU PARTNER AS YOU UNDRESS, DRAW CLOSER, TEMPT HER TO TOUCH YOU AND MOVE AWAY. GIVE A KISS BUT NOTHING ELSE.

4 SHRUG OFF THE JACKET AND THROW IT ASIDE. UNBUTTON YOUR SHIRT SLOWLY AND LEAVE IT HANGING OPEN.

5 UNDO YOUR BELT, SLIDE IT OUT OF YOUR TROUSERS AND THROW IT ASIDE WITH A FLOURISH.

6 TAKE OFF YOUR SHIRT, HOLD IT OVER YOUR SHOULDER, AND DANCE FOR A WHILE, USING IT AS A PROP, TRAILING IT OVER YOUR BODY.

7 DISCARD THE SHIRT, THEN SLOWLY AND TEASINGLY UNDO YOUR FLIES, TURN AROUND AND DROP YOUR TROUSERS TO THE FLOOR.

8 KICK THEM ASIDE QUICKLY, AND TURN ROUND WITH YOUR HANDS COVERING YOUR UNDERWEAR (A POSING POUCH OR BOXER SHORTS, WHICHEVER YOU FEEL COMFORTABLE WITH).

9 TURN YOUR BACK, HOOK YOUR FINGERS INTO THE SIDES, AND PUSH YOUR UNDERPANTS TO THE FLOOR. KICK THEM ASIDE, COVER YOUR PENIS AND TURN BACK.

10 FINALLY, THROW YOUR ARMS IN THE AIR – IT'S THE FULL MONTY!

You can use lingerie to play out different fantasies. Start a dressing-up box and include: a black PVC g-string or mini skirt for bad girl or dominatrix fantasies; a white camisole and French knickers for virginal days; and maybe a Moulin Rouge style basque for when you're feeling flirty and French (ooh lah lah!).

MEN DON'T HAVE QUITE THE SAME RANGE OF SEDUCTIVE UNDERWEAR, BUT PLAIN BOXERS AND BUM-HUGGING TRUNKS ARE VERY ACCEPTABLE. YOU CAN BE MORE ADVENTUROUS IF YOU LIKE: TRY THONGS – PERHAPS LEATHER 'LACE-UPS' FOR EASY FRONTAL ACCESS – OR A TASTEFUL STRING VEST. SHOP AROUND ONLINE FOR IDEAS. ASK YOURSELF 'WHAT WOULD JAMES BOND WEAR?'.

TOP 10 SEXY OUTFITS FOR WOMEN

1 MATCHING LACE BRA OR CAMISOLE TOP, AND KNICKERS – THE FULL SET OF LACY UNDERWEAR COMES IN HUNDREDS OF VARIATIONS, ALL OF THEM GOOD.

2 STOCKINGS, EITHER HOLD-UP OR SUSPENDER – BECAUSE HE CAN RUN HIS HAND UP TO THE TOP AND ENCOUNTER BARE FLESH.

3 SEE-THROUGH NIGHTIES – CAN BE LONG AND ELEGANT OR SHORT AND SWEET BUT ARE ALL VERY SEXY.

4 BASQUES – HOLD YOU IN ALL THE RIGHT PLACES, MAKE YOUR CLEAVAGE FANTASTIC AND YOUR WAIST TINY.

5 CATSUITS – FOR THE CATWOMAN LOOK, A FANTASY SHARED BY COUNTLESS BOYS WHO HAVE BECOME THE MEN YOU'RE SLEEPING WITH.

6 PVC – BECAUSE IT'S TACTILE, SLIMMING AND VERY SLIGHTLY S&M.

7 SHEER DRESSING GOWN – FOR THE 'BORED HOUSEWIFE' LOOK. WEAR WITH FLUFFY MULES AND NOTHING UNDERNEATH.

8 HIGH-HEEL SHOES – LENGTHEN THE LEGS, MAKE YOUR BUM STICK OUT AND ADD SEX APPEAL TO ANY OUTFIT.

9 NURSE OR MAID OUTFIT – MOST MEN GET OFF ON THE IDEA OF BEING SERVICED. IT'S UP TO YOU HOW YOU DO IT.

10 MATCHING VEST AND KNICKERS – CUTE, GIRLISH AND SURPRISINGLY SEXY, UNLESS YOU'RE OVER 45.

Getting It On

GOOD SELF-ESTEEM IS ESSENTIAL
TO FEELING LIKE A RED HOT
SEX GOD OR GODDESS.
DON'T WORRY ABOUT
WHETHER YOUR PARTNER THINKS
YOU'RE FAT OR THAT THEY DON'T
LIKE YOUR NEW HAIRSTYLE. THEY
WOULDN'T BE IN THE SAME BED AS
YOU IF THEY DIDN'T FANCY YOU – IT'S
THE WHOLE PACKAGE THAT THEY WANT.
AND, WHEN YOU SHOW THAT YOU ARE THE
KING OR QUEEN OF LURVE, THEY WILL WANT
YOU EVEN MORE!

Take it in turns to say positive things about each other. Tell your partner what you like about them so that they feel as good as you do: 'you are so sexy… I love nibbling behind those ears and feeling your body rise to mine…'. But try to be honest about what you think – honest but sexy – without sounding like a bad porno novel.

Practice makes perfect. And of all the things that you could have to practice, what could be more fun? When you try something new, remember, it's new for your partner too. Take your time so that both you and your partner feel at ease. Learn to laugh at yourself. So what if you make a mistake in bed or out? Your partner isn't keeping score on a giant flipchart!

Look the best you can and you'll feel good – get a great haircut, brush your teeth, keep your nails clean and keep your skin moisturised all over.

TOP 10 ATMOSPHERIC TIPS

1 LIGHT LOTS OF CANDLES, NOT JUST ONE OR TWO –
BUY CHEAP TEA LIGHTS AND LIGHT 50 INSTEAD OF
TURNING THE LIGHTS ON.

2 BURN ESSENTIAL OIL IN A BURNER, OR SPRINKLE A
FEW DROPS ON THE RADIATOR.

3 USE GIANT FLOOR CUSHIONS AND THICK RUGS OR
THROWS TO LIE ON, INSTEAD OF PERCHING ON
CHAIRS.

4 DEPENDING ON HOW WELL YOU KNOW YOUR
PARTNER, YOU MIGHT LIKE TO SETTLE DOWN TO AN
EROTIC FRENCH FILM OR EVEN A SOFT PORN FILM, TO
GET YOU IN THE MOOD.

5 KEEP THE HEATING COMFORTABLY WARM – BEING CHILLY IS NEVER SEXY. A REAL FIRE IS BEST OF ALL.

6 PLAY LOUNGE MUSIC – IT'S EASY TO LISTEN TO AND DOESN'T HAVE THE SWEEPING, EMOTIONAL MOVEMENTS OF CLASSICAL MUSIC, WHICH CAN CHANGE THE ATMOSPHERE TOO SUDDENLY.

7 IF YOU'RE NOT USING CANDLES, ALWAYS HAVE LAMPS, NEVER AN OVERHEAD LIGHT.

8 DON'T LEAVE THE TV ON!

9 HAVE FRESH FLOWERS IN VASES DOTTED AROUND – THEY SMELL GREAT, AND ADD COLOUR AND LIFE TO A ROOM.

10 LEAVE SOME EROTIC NOVELS LYING AROUND IN CASE YOU WANT TO READ TO EACH OTHER.

You don't have to remove underwear before you have sex; keeping it on can add to the urgent thrill. G-strings can be pushed to one side (on men too) and bras pulled down.

G-STRINGS LOOK BETTER
THAN KNICKERS ON WOMEN –
THEY HIGHLIGHT THE EROTICISM
OF THE BEAUTIFUL SHAPELY
CURVES OF YOUR BUM.

Men, if you're insecure about your Homer Simpson-style stomachs, keeping a shirt on can be sexy, so long as it's a sexy shirt! You don't have to be naked to have great, passionate sex – in fact, sometimes it helps not to be.

IF YOU DON'T HAVE THE BODY YOU'D LIKE TO HAVE, RESOLVE TO EXERCISE MORE, OR CUT DOWN ON DRINKING. THAT'S A FAR MORE POSITIVE CHOICE THAN RESOLVING TO HIDE IT FROM YOUR PARTNER. AVOIDING SEXUAL INTIMACY ADDS PROBLEMS AND IS GENERALLY JUST NO FUN.

Sex Games

Playing games
together can
spice up your
sex life in ways
you never even
considered. If you feel
a bit inhibited,
remember – games such
as strip poker are simply
gradual undressing games.
Play games just with your
lover for full enjoyment.
Strip Scrabble, anybody?

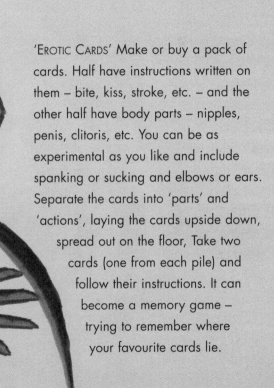

'EROTIC CARDS' Make or buy a pack of cards. Half have instructions written on them – bite, kiss, stroke, etc. – and the other half have body parts – nipples, penis, clitoris, etc. You can be as experimental as you like and include spanking or sucking and elbows or ears. Separate the cards into 'parts' and 'actions', laying the cards upside down, spread out on the floor, Take two cards (one from each pile) and follow their instructions. It can become a memory game – trying to remember where your favourite cards lie.

'POSITION AND LOCATION DICE' Buy two large dice from a toy shop. On pieces of paper small enough to fit on each side of the dice, write six positions, for example, doggy, missionary, etc., and six locations, such as in the car or on the kitchen floor. Stick all the 'positions' on one dice and all the 'locations' on the other. Take turns to roll the dice and follow the instructions – wherever they take you!

'ORGASM COMPETITION' Take turns to arouse each other to the point of no return, and the first one to come (which will almost certainly be the men) is the loser. The winner gets a full night featuring the sex of their choice. And the loser gets to join in.

'LOVE CHEQUES' In sex shops and the gift book section of bookshops, you can find 'love cheques' that promise to pay the bearer on demand everything from a full massage to a blow job. However, whenever one is presented, you have to be prepared to drop everything and cash the cheque.

'EROTIC PHONE-IN' Ring your partner, wherever they may be, with an erotically themed question that must be answered. If he or she gets it wrong, then your lover is destined to do your sexual bidding when they get home. But if they get it right, then you become their sex slave.

'STRIP AND FORFEITS' Forget strip poker – liven up your stripping games with strip crossword, or strip Trivial Pursuit (but not Strip Monopoly, it takes so long you'll be blue with cold by the end!). You can also add forfeits to make it more interesting – kissing or licking tend to work best.

'NAME THAT TASTE' One partner is blindfolded.
The other spreads some kind of food or drink
on their body. and the blindfolded partner has
to lick it off, naming the taste of the food and
the body part. If they guess the food or the
body part incorrectly, a new food or body
part is chosen, until they guess everything
correctly. There really are no losers in this!

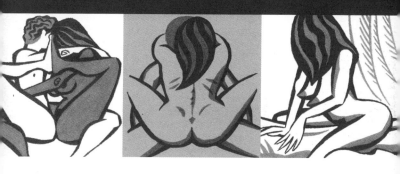

2 TOYS

It's fun to have red hot sex with nothing but your naked selves. But even before you get bored, consider spicing up life with the addition of some sex toys. Your sex play can be longer and your orgasms mind blowing. As long as they don't become a substitute for communication between you, they can enhance your sexual activity and turn the whole experience from 'OK' to 'red hot' in minutes.

Vibrators

Vibrators work for both women and men.
They aren't just a penis-substitute, but are for
the boys too – placing a lightly buzzing wand against
his sensitive shaft can ensure that by the time it's
rubbed slowly over the tip, he'll be ready to explode.

YOU CAN BUY YOUR VIBRATOR FROM
MAIL-ORDER CATALOGUES OR OVER
THE INTERNET, SO YOU'LL NO LONGER
SUFFER THE EMBARRASSMENT OF
HAVING TO SHUFFLE ROUND A SEX
SHOP, TRYING NOT TO CATCH THE
PROPRIETOR'S EYE.

71

You can choose electric or battery-powered vibrators. Battery-powered are less powerful but manoeuvrable – just don't let the batteries run out at a crucial moment! Electric vibrators are a lot less discreet and need to be near a mains socket, but they give a good buzz.

A NEW QUIETER MODEL, THE WHISPER, HAS RECENTLY BEEN LAUNCHED, WHICH NOT ONLY VIBRATES, BUT ALSO EMITS A DEEP THROBBING PULSE THAT CLAIMS TO GUARANTEE FEMALE ORGASM.

Most vibrators have two speeds.
Start slowly and increase speed
as you get increasingly excited,
or simply keep it switched to
one rhythm, moving it
around in small circles.

YOU CAN HOLD AND GENTLY RUB A
VIBRATOR AGAINST YOUR NIPPLES,
BALANCE IT BETWEEN PENIS AND
VAGINA DURING INTERCOURSE SO
IT STIMULATES HIS SHAFT AND HER
CLITORIS SIMULTANEOUSLY, OR HE
CAN USE IT TO HELP HER COME
WHEN HIS FINGERS AND TONGUE
ARE FINALLY EXHAUSTED.

MEN ARE HUGELY TURNED ON BY WATCHING THEIR PARTNERS USE A VIBRATOR. IF A WOMAN IS PREPARED TO MASTURBATE IN FRONT OF HER LOVER, SHE CAN DRIVE HIM WILD WITHOUT EVEN TOUCHING HIM.

Vibrators stimulate the male prostate more effectively than fingers. Use lots of lubricant then gently push it into the anus. When it is all the way in, or just before, switch it on to slow and, as arousal increases and orgasm starts to arrive, increase the speed. This will enhance orgasm but might hasten its arrival. And be aware ladies, that not all men will want you to do this to them.

77

ALWAYS TREAT YOUR VIBRATOR WELL AND CLEAN THOROUGHLY WITH SOAP AND WATER AFTER EVERY USE. YOU AND YOUR LOVER MIGHT HAVE ONE EACH OR YOU MIGHT USE A CONDOM ON IT (JUST LIKE A REAL PENIS) FOR EXTRA SAFETY.

Ladies, did you know that you can get a very small vibrator that can clip to your knickers and, whenever you flick the switch (and some are remote control) you will get a buzz against your clitoris? Sounds fun? Just hold your facial expressions in check during those long, arduous business meetings… Men, what a great present for your partner.

TOP 10 VIBRATORS

1 THE *RAMPANT RABBIT*: MOST POPULAR OF ALL, IT OFFERS A CLITORAL STIMULATOR AND GYRATING BEADS.

2 *NATURAL CONTOURS*: DESIGNED BY A WOMAN, IT IS SHAPED LIKE A BENDY ELECTRIC RAZOR AND FITS RIGHT OVER YOUR PUBIC BONE TO PRESS ON THE CLITORIS.

3 THE *DEEP SPACE* VIBRATOR: VERY HI-TECH, WITH A STYLISH SILVER ATTACHMENT THAT CAN STIMULATE YOU INTERNALLY AND EXTERNALLY.

4 THE *BASIC WAND*: BEST IN SILVER OR GOLD, RATHER THAN FLESH-COLOURED. THE WAND OFFERS A GENTLE BUT EFFECTIVE BUZZ.

5 *LOVE EGGS*: TWO SOFT, SPIKY BALLS. INSERT THEM AND ALLOW THE SILICON PRICKLES TO STIMULATE THE PARTS THAT OTHER VIBRATORS CAN'T REACH.

6 THE *FINGER TICKLER*: A SIMPLE ATTACHMENT THAT CLIPS TO THE FINGER AND VIBRATES WITH A TINY BATTERY.

7 THERE ARE VIBRATORS THAT ARE THE SIZE AND SHAPE OF LIPSTICKS THAT YOU CAN POP IN YOUR HANDBAG FOR UNEXPECTED ENCOUNTERS!

8 *BUTTERFLY*: A TINY DISC WITH A BATTERY THAT CLIPS INTO YOUR KNICKERS AND DELIVERS A CONTINUOUS THRILL.

9 *ELECTRONIC*: VIBRATORS THAT PLUG IN OFFER A DEEPER, MORE INTENSE THRILL, BUT ARE OFTEN LESS SUBTLE.

10 THE *WHISPER*: IS A NEW MODEL THAT CLAIMS TO THROB, RATHER THAN PULSE, AND BARELY MAKES A NOISE AT ALL.

The normal sized vibrator styles are available in the following options:

- ▸ the wand (most basic, plain style), perhaps with a rotating head
- ▸ a wand style with clit stimulator attached
- ▸ a wand with a clit stimulator and a tiny extension that puts pressure on the anus
- ▸ a wand style with beads in the central shaft that rotate
- ▸ or any combination of these

DILDOS ARE SIMPLY SEX TOYS IN THE SHAPE OF A PENIS, OFTEN MADE FROM SILICON RUBBER MATERIALS. THEY CAN BE USED TO PENETRATE THE ANUS AND, FOR THE GIRLS, COME WITH A STRAP-ON HARNESS.

You can get double-ended dildos that can be twice the fun by using it in his anus and in her vagina at the same time (or any other variation that you'd like to try). Again, always wash thoroughly after use.

Hand- And Wrist Cuffs

A little light bondage can be a great sexual game, but unless both of you are equally keen, don't even go there. You need total trust in order to relax properly, so it's definitely not a pastime for a one-night stand.

HANDCUFFS JOIN THE HANDS TOGETHER, WHEREAS WRIST CUFFS HAVE RINGS THAT ALLOW YOU TO TIE THEM TO OBJECTS, SUCH AS THE BEDPOST. IF YOU WANT TO GO ALL THE WAY, THERE ARE ANKLE CUFFS TOO!

Don't lie on the bed with your arms tied behind you, because that's not a turn-on and your arms will hurt. Much sexier is to be spread-eagled on the bed, with each wrist tied above your head, and both ankles fastened to the bottom of the bed. This will make you feel vulnerable, but is very erotic and your partner has total freedom to do whatever they like to you.

TOP 5 BONDAGE TIPS

1 PADDED HANDCUFFS AND WRIST CUFFS ARE THE MOST COMFORTABLE FORM OF RESTRAINT.

2 DON'T LOCK WRISTS BEHIND THE BACK BECAUSE IT STRAINS THE SHOULDERS PAINFULLY.

3 USE SCARVES INSTEAD OF CUFFS BUT ALWAYS CHOOSE SILK BECAUSE IT IS MORE COMFORTABLE.

4 NEVER, EVER, PUT THE KEY IN A 'SAFE PLACE' AND FORGET WHERE YOU PUT IT.

5 AGREE ON A WORD THAT MEANS 'STOP AND LET ME OUT' IN ADVANCE (DON'T JUST USE 'STOP' BECAUSE THIS MIGHT BE USED IN THE REGULAR COURSE OF YOUR PASSION).

Women can be tied at the wrists and assume the doggy position – slightly undignified for her (but it'll feel great), and very sexy for him. It gives deep penetration and the man's shaft rubs against the pelvis, oral sex is great, and he can stimulate her with his fingers. He can also reach round to her breasts.

Sit on a chair with your ankles bound to each chair leg, and your arms tied loosely behind the back of the chair. Ladies, you can mount your man and tease him, and men, you can give your partner lots of licking. (Make sure it's a sturdy piece of furniture!)

Fantasy is a much-enjoyed accompaniment to bondage scenarios, such as:

▶ Naughty schoolgirl and wicked headmaster

▶ Roman Slave and Slave-owner

▶ Wicked nurse and captive patient

Or use your own sexy ideas.

Standing up, fasten his wrists (loosely) behind his back, or to a four poster bed, and give him oral sex. He'll be unable to touch you – frustrating yet deeply, erotically charged.

When your partner's tied up, they're in your power, so use a variety of touches and caresses to drive them wild. Light, feathery stroking all over works for women. For men, who prefer a firmer touch, sweep your fingers over his chest and work your way down to his penis. Avoid touching it until he's begging. Cover your partner's body with kisses, circle your tongue on their nipples and trail it right down to their pubic bone. Then work your way back up again, after kissing and licking their inner thighs.

Nipple Clamps

Nipple clamps are small metal clips that fix to your nipples, and can come with linking chains that add to the 'bondage' experience. They stimulate the nipples through (varying degrees of) pain and this can be a very intense erotic experience, working best when other areas of the body are being stimulated. If you're not used to these, start with adjustable clamps, with a fairly light grip.

Use your fingers to lightly squeeze your lover's nipples during sex, sometimes pulling them away from the body, and check out your partner's reaction. Gradually squeeze a bit harder, as long as your partner is comfortable. Fingers work just as well as clamps, but they stop your hands from concentrating on other things!

Spanking

Spanking, usually on the bum, stimulates through pain and, like nipples clamps, can provide great intensity of, and more wide-spread, feeling. Using a small wooden bat has the same effect as spanking with your hand, whereas whips tend to sting a little more. You might find that you can use both during your lovemaking.

Place your lover with their bum in a good position (retaining access to as much of the rest of their body as possible) and, using your hands at first, slap them lightly on the bum. Keep the slap rhythmic and stop frequently to caress and fondle other parts of your partner's body. If you have a bat, you might like to use this if you decide to slap a little harder. Gradually introduce the whip, gently, and use it to tease your lover by dragging it up and down their body and over their genitals. Give a few rhythmic light lashes and tease a bit, fondle your partner occasionally, and gradually increase the intensity. Always be sensitive to your lover's reactions and ensure that they're content.

Blindfold

YOU CAN USE ANYTHING FOR A BLINDFOLD – FROM A SILK SCARF TO A TO A FULL LEATHER FACEMASK. THE SENSATION OF TOUCHING IS HEIGHTENED BECAUSE YOUR PARTNER WILL BE ON TENTERHOOKS WONDERING WHERE YOU'RE GOING TO TOUCH NEXT AND, BECAUSE THEY CAN'T SEE, YOUR LOVER CAN CONCENTRATE ON, AND ENJOY MORE FULLY, YOUR CARESSES, KISSES AND LICKS.

With your lover on their back, cover their eyes with a blindfold. Start by licking their earlobes and sensitive parts of their neck. Work your way down their body, kissing, licking and touching the breasts or nipples, down towards the genitals (touch, but don't go too far at this point). Continue towards the inside of the thighs. Your partner should be squirming under your touch by now. You can now continue by giving oral sex, just teasing them, or taking off the blindfold and enjoying some more games.

TOP 10 TOY BOX

1 CONDOMS!

2 THE VERSATILE VIBRATOR – THE MORE TYPES YOU HAVE, THE MORE FUN YOU CAN HAVE WITH THEM.

3 LUBRICANT – FRUITY AND SLIPPERY.

4 SEXY BLINDFOLD – BLACK SILK OR A FULL-ON LEATHER MASK IF YOU WANT TO BE MORE DRAMATIC.

5 MASSAGE OIL MADE FROM SENSUAL OILS.

6 FURRY HANDCUFFS OR BLACK LEATHER WRIST AND ANKLE CUFFS (AND A LENGTH OF ROPE FOR ATTACHING THEM TO THINGS!).

7 SMALL CAT O' NINE TAILS WHIP, LONG ENOUGH TO TEASE, SHORT ENOUGH SO THAT YOU DON'T TAKE YOUR EYE OUT WHEN YOU'RE USING IT.

8 BUM BEADS – JUST FOR HIM.

9 WHATEVER YOU NEED TO CARRY OUT YOUR FANTASY GAME – NURSES HAT, FEATHER BOA, ETC.

10 VIDEOS – A BIT OF SOFT PORN OR EROTIC FRENCH FILM TO GET YOU IN THE MOOD.

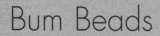

Bum Beads

This is a small string of beads. Push them up his bum, leaving the end of the string hanging out. As he approaches the moment of climax, pull the string for a prostate stimulation he'll never forget.

Gags

If you want to try gags, be very careful indeed. Buy one specially made for the purpose, as a homemade one may prove highly dangerous, and you don't want to end your sex session looking up 'resuscitate' in the medical handbook.

Cock Rings

The cock ring is a little rubber ring with a hole in the middle. It may have an attachment to stimulate her clitoris while he's wearing it. It maintains the blood in his erection, so he's as big and hard as possible.

VARIOUS RUBBER FINGER-ATTACHMENTS THAT LOOK LIKE KNOBBLY THIMBLES CLAIM TO STIMULATE THE CLITORIS, BUT IT'S DEBATABLE WHETHER ANY DO A BETTER JOB THAN A VIBRATOR.

Food

Food is fantastic to play
with during sex – it's
sensuous, slippery and juicy
and is sure to bring out the
animal in you. An important rule
is don't play with anything that
might get stuck and watch out for
spicy and citrus food near
your sensitive parts!

GIVE YOUR PARTNER A CAN OF
DREAMY CREAM AND ASK HER TO
SQUIRT THE CREAM WHERE SHE'D
LIKE TO HAVE IT LICKED OFF. THIS
MAKES IT MORE FUN AND SEXY
FOR BOTH OF YOU. THEN ASK
HER TO SQUIRT IT ON YOU...

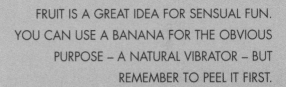

FRUIT IS A GREAT IDEA FOR SENSUAL FUN. YOU CAN USE A BANANA FOR THE OBVIOUS PURPOSE – A NATURAL VIBRATOR – BUT REMEMBER TO PEEL IT FIRST.

Eat cherries from her vagina (but don't get them lost up there) and balance pineapple rings on his penis then nibble them off. All small, sweet fruits are good for eating off one another's bodies – particularly strawberries, raspberries and grapes.

TOP 5 FOOD FOR THOUGHT

1 CHOCOLATE – GO FOR CHOCOLATE PAINTS OR CHOCOLATE SPREAD.

2 FRUITS – MIX UP THE JUICE OF SOFT, SQUIDGY STRAWBERRIES, GRAPES, MANGO, PINEAPPLE AND RASPBERRIES WITH YOUR OWN NATURAL JUICES.

3 ICE CREAM – LET THE COLD CONTRAST AND CREAMY TEXTURE SEDUCE YOU.

4 HONEY – IT DRIPS, IT SLIDES, IT'S STICKY, IT'S GREAT.

5 PEANUT BUTTER AND JAM – A PERFECT SANDWICH WITH YOUR PARTNER!

Chocolate contains a chemical thought to mimic the sensation of falling in love – so it's the ideal substance to use on each other. Invest in some chocolate body paint and get creative!

An ice-cold ice cube against
the warm body is a very erotic
sensation, for both of you.

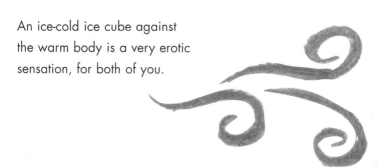

You can (carefully) slide the cube, using your hand

or your mouth, anywhere you like, slowly dripping melted ice as you go.

TOP 10 APHRODISIACS

1 ASPARAGUS – PHALLIC SHAPE, SEXY TASTE.

2 GRAPES – THE GREEK GOD DIONYSUS WAS NOT ONLY THE GOD OF WINE BUT ALSO THE GOD OF FERTILITY AND PROCREATION.

3 LIQUORICE – IN TESTS, MEN WERE PROVED TO HAVE INCREASED PENILE BLOOD FLOW WHEN EXPOSED TO THE SMELL OF LIQUORICE.

4 OYSTERS – PACKED WITH ZINC, A SEX-DRIVE BOOSTING CHEMICAL.

5 PINE NUTS – AN ACKNOWLEDGED APHRODISIAC, DATING AS FAR BACK AS ANCIENT THE POET, OVID.

6 GARLIC – ONCE CONSIDERED IRRESISTIBLY APHRODISIAC, ONE ANCIENT RECIPE INVOLVED GARLIC AND LARD RUBBED ON TO THE PENIS.

7 TRUFFLES – A RICH, RARE FUNGUS, APPARENTLY CONTAINING A HUGE SEXUAL KICK.

8 LOBSTER – A SEAFOOD RICH IN PHOSPHOROUS AND IODINE, WHICH IS GOOD FOR BLOOD FLOW.

9 HONEY – PACKED WITH CARBOHYDRATE, WHICH IMPROVES STAMINA.

10 CUCUMBER – THE SCENT IS APPARENTLY ENOUGH TO INCREASE BLOOD FLOW TO THE VITAL REGIONS.

Champagne is the sexiest drink in the world. Buy the best you can afford, and pour it onto each other. The tingling sensation feels incredible on the genitals, and you must lick it off afterwards so you don't waste any.

You can kiss it between each others' mouths, or drizzle it over her breasts. Its effects make you feel like the sexiest individual in the world – erotic, confident and willing to try anything – and the sheer decadence of the expense is enough to make you feel like a wild child.

3 FOREPLAY

Foreplay is the difference between OK and red hot sex. It isn't just for women – good foreplay can enhance a man's sexual experience so much, he almost won't care about penetration.

Kissing

If you can't kiss, you can't have great sex either. Begin with closed lips, parted gently, and then brush across the surface of your partner's lips. Only when the passion is building should you allow your tongue to flick in and out of your partner's mouth.

WITH THE TIP OF YOUR TONGUE.

Nibble and suck lightly on both top and bottom lips. Hindus believe there's a nerve that links the upper lip to the genitals, so make the most of it. Kiss your partner all over their face, alternating light, feathery touches with bolder, more intense brushes of your lips.

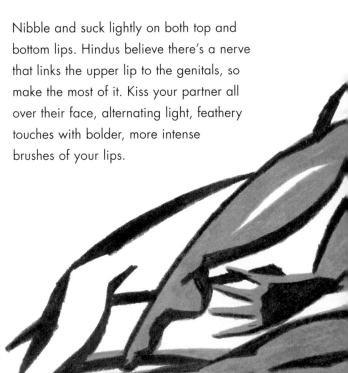

Hot and cold liquids will intensify the eroticism of your kiss.

Don't behave as though you're performing a tonsillectomy. When the kiss becomes passionate, withdraw your tongue slightly and allow your mouth to slide across your partner's, stimulating all the sensitive nerve endings.

ORAL HYGIENE IS VITAL. NEVER ATTEMPT TO KISS UNLESS YOU'VE BRUSHED YOUR TEETH RECENTLY AND USED BREATH-FRESHENER AND LIP BALM TO MAKE SURE YOUR MOUTH IS SOFT AND WELCOMING.

A great way to practise your kissing is to agree with your partner to kiss for as long as you can – not just squeezing your lips together, but any kind of tender tongue and lip touches that you can think of. You might make it kisses only or tongues only, and see what develops.

Although men are genitally centred, everyone has their favourite places to be kissed – often well be away from the usual erogenous zones. So kiss away, but if there's no response, move on.

Kissing isn't restricted to the face. You can kiss everywhere, particularly erogenous zones including the back of the knees, earlobes, neck, bum, breasts or chest and hands. Some people love to have their feet kissed, but some kick like an Arab stallion in horror at the very idea, so check first.

Seduction

Slide your hand down to the open neck or collar of your partner's top. Trail your fingers up and down, as if about to lift if off or undo a button. Tease for a while, before you peel the article of clothing from them your partner's body.

Leave your lover's bra in place for a while, lightly tracing your fingers over her breasts through the fabric to titillate her, then slide one strap off her shoulder and kiss her collar bone and neck.

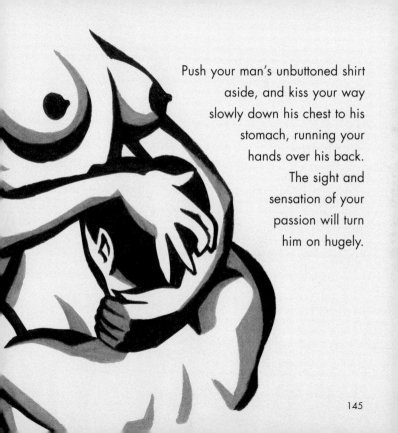

Push your man's unbuttoned shirt aside, and kiss your way slowly down his chest to his stomach, running your hands over his back. The sight and sensation of your passion will turn him on hugely.

BITING CAN BE EROTIC,
AS LONG AS IT'S GENTLE,
LIGHT NIBBLING RATHER
THAN VAMPIRE-LIKE NECK
GOUGING. DELICATE
PRESSURE STIMULATES THE
NERVES, PARTICULARLY
AROUND THE EARS,
JAW AND NECK.

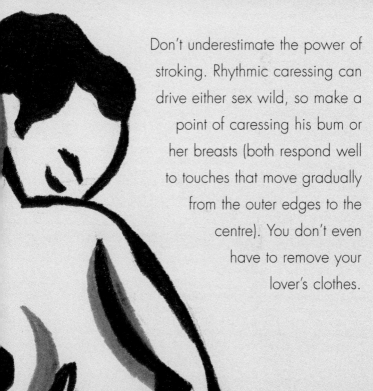

Don't underestimate the power of stroking. Rhythmic caressing can drive either sex wild, so make a point of caressing his bum or her breasts (both respond well to touches that move gradually from the outer edges to the centre). You don't even have to remove your lover's clothes.

If you lick your partner's ear, be careful to do it quietly because it's not erotic if it sounds like a washing machine chewing your ear.

Licking (and kissing) all over the body is a great bedroom turn-on. Avoid lapping like a dog – just flicker your tongue across skin occasionally.

Foreplay And Your Woman

The way in which you touch your partner's genitals can make all the difference. Do it the wrong way and you'll be there for hours, wondering where you went wrong. Do it the right way, though, and she'll be your sex slave forever.

WHEN YOU BEGIN TO TOUCH YOUR LOVER, REMOVE HER KNICKERS SLOWLY. YOU CAN TOY WITH HER FOR A BIT, CARESSING AND TEASING THROUGH HER UNDERWEAR, BEFORE CAREFULLY UNPEELING HER KNICKERS FROM HER BODY.

151

Rub massage oil or lube into your hands and, fingers pointing towards her bum, place your fingers on her labia and draw your hands towards her belly button, one hand then the other. As you go, move your hand and fingers to explore the inner and outer labia. Stop occasionaly and gently tug or rub the outer lips between your thumb and forefinger.

Slide your fore- or middle finger onto her labia, without pressure. Stroke it for a while, running your hand back and forth. Make sure she's turned on by increasing the pressure slightly around her vagina. If she's not wet, she's not ready for you to touch her clitoris just yet, so keep stroking the whole area for a few more minutes. If she is, you can gently part her labia and place two fingers alongside her clitoris. For those who don't know (and you should make it your business to find out), it's usually located at the point where her legs close together, but if you're unsure, it feels like a small pea under the skin.

Rub the clitoris very gently in small circles, with a steady rhythm. There's a technique called the 'clit clock' in which you make very small circles with your finger, stopping briefly each time you reach '12 o'clock'.

Remember men, woman are
sensitive all over their bodies –
much more so than men – so,
as you're playing with her down
below, don't forget to (carefully)
kiss, stroke and touch her.
The more sensation she feels,
the more she'll react.

MOVE ONE OR TWO FINGERS, OR A VIBRATOR, IN AND OUT OF HER VAGINA WHILE YOU RUB HER CLITORIS OR JUST STROKE GENTLY AT THE ENTRANCE – AS SOME WOMEN FIND TWO-POINT STIMULATION A LITTLE TOO DISTRACTING. SOME WOMEN LIKE THREE-POINT STIMULATION, WITH A FINGER ON THE CLITORIS, VAGINA AND ANUS AT THE SAME TIME. IF YOU CAN MANAGE TO TOUCH YOUR LOVER'S NIPPLES AS WELL, SHE'LL EXPLODE.

Insert your first two fingers into your lover's vagina. Arch your thumb back (a bit like a hitchhiker might) and rest it against her clitoris. Thrust or twist your fingers, or simply vibrate your whole hand.

THE MORE YOU KNOW YOUR LOVER, THE EASIER
IT WILL BECOME TO UNDERSTAND WHAT TURNS
HER ON. HOWEVER, EVERY WOMAN TAKES A
DIFFERENT AMOUNT OF TIME TO BECOME
ORGASMICALLY STIMULATED – FROM FIVE
MINUTES TO AN HOUR – SO BE PREPARED!

If your partner has a certain 'spot' that
they liked caressed or licked, just play
around this area touching the 'hot' spot
occasionally. The teasing will heighten
the feeling of this sensitive area.

Foreplay And Your Man

To give your man a great hand-job, grip his penis as if you're holding a glass of beer – firmly but not hard enough to shatter it. Use your whole fist, and move your hand up and down right to the head and back, gradually increasing in speed. If your hand is lubricated, it'll stimulate the shaft. If he's circumcised (that is, he has no foreskin) use the same movement, but don't pull at the skin – a drop of lube can help to minimise friction.

Using both hands will provide a novel sensation for your lover, particularly if you lubricate them first. Link your fingers loosely over the tip of his penis, and rub your palms up and down the shaft.

The most sensitive part is the frenulum, the piece of skin that joins head to shaft. Use the ball of your thumb to stroke it gently, and rub lightly alongside the vein that runs up the front of his erect penis.

Don't squeeze too hard on the shaft, but don't grip too loosely either – he needs to feel the friction you're generating with your hand. Build up gradually, or your elbow will go numb before he's come.

'THE TWIST' Lubricate your hands and hold his penis with your thumb and forefinger together at the bottom. Stroke upwards, performing a little twisting motion when you reach the top. Start again and keep stroking and twisting – not too hard – for a unique thrill.

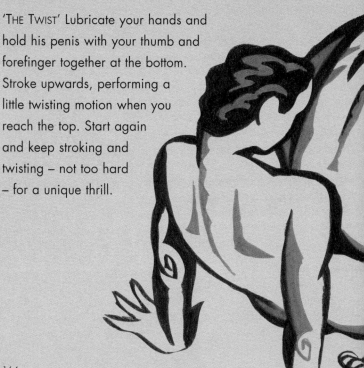

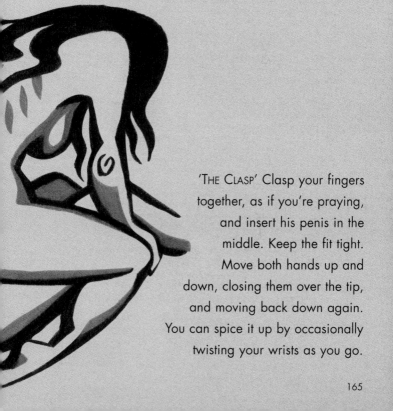

'THE CLASP' Clasp your fingers together, as if you're praying, and insert his penis in the middle. Keep the fit tight. Move both hands up and down, closing them over the tip, and moving back down again. You can spice it up by occasionally twisting your wrists as you go.

'THE PULL' Lubricate your hands. Now perform long, alternate strokes on his penis, starting from the balls and gently pulling his penis upwards. This is a good technique to get him going because if he's not erect, he soon will be.

Don't ignore his balls –
they are highly sensitive and while you
must never bite, pinch or otherwise be
brutal with them, they respond
exceptionally well to light licking, sucking
and stroking while you touch his penis.

Grasp his penis firmly in one hand
and move the shaft up and down.
With your other hand, cup his
balls and pull lightly down-
wards. You're setting up a
lovely sensation of friction,
so when you move your
hand down the shaft, stop
pulling, and when you
move it back up, tug lightly.
Just remember to keep your
hand movements steady.

Circle the tip of your tongue tip on his penis, then flick it back and forth like a sensual python. Return to his perineum (the piece of skin between his balls and his anus) and run your tongue firmly along it, rotating the tip when he groans with passion.

If you can, suck gently on his balls until they're entirely inside your mouth. This gives him a delightfully warm, enclosed, sexy feeling – it's not as intense as having his penis sucked, it's a gentler sensation.

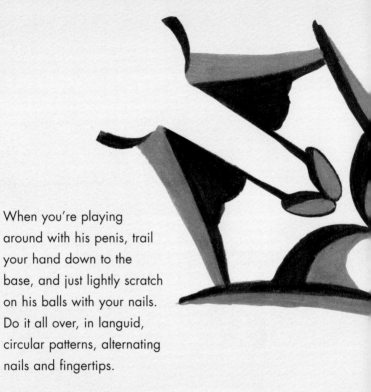

When you're playing around with his penis, trail your hand down to the base, and just lightly scratch on his balls with your nails. Do it all over, in languid, circular patterns, alternating nails and fingertips.

172

The perineum responds very well to gentle but firm pressure. If you press it just as he's about to come, it will intensify his orgasm. Don't prod by mistake, or he'll scream with pain, not pleasure.

TOP 5 TOUCHING HER

1 NIPPLES – THERE'S A DIRECT LINE OF SENSITIVITY TO HER GENITALS.

2 VAGINA – OBVIOUSLY.

3 ANUS – ENHANCES THE SENSATIONS SHE'S FEELING.

4 CLITORIS – USE YOUR FINGERS TO ENHANCE WHAT YOUR MOUTH'S DOING.

5 BUM – KNEAD AND SQUEEZE IT AS YOU LICK HER.

Oral Sex For Her

Oral sex can be part of foreplay or a lovely way to make your lover orgasm. And even if you're not that great a lover in other respects, if you can get your girl writhing with ecstasy using oral sex, she will love you forever.

MANY MEN MAKE THE MISTAKE OF ATTACKING THEIR PARTNER'S CLITORIS AS THOUGH IT'S A MELTING ICE LOLLY. YOU NEED TO BE MUCH MORE GENTLE, PARTING HER LABIA A LITTLE SO THAT YOU CAN SEE WHAT YOU'RE DOING, AND CIRCLING THE TIP OF YOUR TONGUE AROUND THE CLITORIS.

If you don't yet know what your lover enjoys, hold open the labia and start by moving your tongue from her vagina to her clitoris. Run it along the folds, circling it at the entrance of the vagina, or flick your tongue back and forth at the very edge of her clitoris.

LICKING ANYWHERE IN THE GENITAL AREA WILL FEEL PRETTY GOOD, BUT DON'T BE AFRAID TO ASK IF IT'S IN THE RIGHT PLACE IF YOU'RE NOT SURE. WHEN YOU FIND A TOUCH SHE LIKES, STICK WITH IT (BUT CONTINUE TO EXPERIMENT).

Most women like the tongue to be loose as it slides over the clitoris, but you can also make your tongue into a point. Open the lips, and gently flick the clitoris, with your tongue occasionally roaming around the other secret places in between times.

You might like to take the clitoris in your mouth and very gently suck and pull ever so slightly, sliding off to lick some more. This can be particularly effective if your partner's really hot.

Once you've started, keep up a steady pace – there's nothing worse than getting her to the brink of orgasm, then suddenly shifting position and rhythm altogether. Slow and steady is great, with increases of speed to take it a bit further now and again.

USE YOUR FINGERS TO SUPPLEMENT
YOUR MOVEMENTS, STROKING THE
ENTRANCE TO THE VAGINA, AND IF
YOUR LOVER LIKES IT, SLIDE YOUR
TONGUE IN AND OUT AND KEEP
UP THE STIMULATION WITH
YOUR FINGERS.

Don't stop the moment she
begins to orgasm – she may
need a final move to push
her over the edge. When
she's finished, she'll let
you know!

182

TOP 5 POSITIONS FOR ORAL SEX (For Both Of You!)

1 THE CLASSIC – HE LIES ON HIS BACK, SHE LIES WITH HER HEAD BETWEEN HIS LEGS.

2 SHE LIES ON HER BACK AND HE LIES AT RIGHT ANGLES – LESS CLAUSTROPHOBIC FOR HIM, AND HER LEGS ARE FREE TO THRASH WITH PASSION.

3 SHE SITS JUST ABOVE HIS FACE – DIFFICULT TO BALANCE AT THE MOMENT OF ORGASM, BUT VERY EROTIC.

4 HE SITS ON A CHAIR OR STANDS AND SHE
KNEELS BETWEEN HIS LEGS.

5 69 – WELL, IF YOU DON'T KNOW WHAT THIS
IS... BOTH OF YOU LYING DOWN, WITH EACH
PARTNER'S HEAD FACING THE OTHER'S GENITALS.

Oral Sex For Him

GRASP THE BASE OF HIS PENIS WITH ONE HAND, HIS BALLS IN THE OTHER, AND BEGIN TO MOVE YOUR MOUTH UP AND DOWN, ONLY TAKING IN AS MUCH OF HIS PENIS AS YOU'RE COMFORT-ABLE WITH. ANGLE YOUR HEAD SO THAT THE END OF HIS PENIS HITS YOUR CHEEK.

With your lips on the tip, breathe gently over his penis, blowing on him. Lick from the bottom of the shaft upwards – the large vein that runs along the inside is particularly sensitive.

Make his penis wet all over using your tongue (the wetter the better), and play with him using your hands.

Don't forget to play with his balls during fellatio, perhaps scratching them gently with your fingernails.

USE YOUR FINGERS TO CARESS HIS BALLS, PERINEUM AND HIS ANUS, IF HE LIKES IT, WHILE YOU SUCK HIM. THIS KIND OF TOUCHING WILL INTENSIFY HIS SENSATION AND MAKE HIM COME MORE QUICKLY.

When the top half of the shaft is in your mouth, keep moving your head up and down, but use your tongue to draw swirls on the head, paying particular attention to the frenulum. If you want to prolong it, you can break off when he gets close to orgasm and run your tongue up and down the vein at the front of his penis. It's very sensitive and delicate so licking up and down its length will drive him wild.

Keep your lips firmly closed around the head of the penis and your teeth tucked away behind your lips. A light suction is required to keep him hard.

When you want to turn up the heat, put your wet lips around the head of the penis and slide them down over his shaft, then suck for a while – sometimes hard, sometimes softly – and repeat the pattern. Twist your head around as you move up and down. Use your hands too – you don't have to give yourself neck ache, bobbing back and forth. Massage the head when you have his whole penis in your mouth, using the flat of your tongue to slide on and off.

4 TALKING **DIRTY**

Talking dirty is a great way to add a bit of fun and fantasy (and variation) into sex or to make a lacklustre sex life sparkle again. But first, you have to overcome any inhibitions about sounding silly or making a fool of yourself. Performed with confidence, dirty talk will become effortless and will sound very, very sexy.

KEEP YOUR DIRTYTALK SHORT AND TO THE POINT. YOU CAN BE LOVING, BUT BEING POETIC IS FOR ROMANCE, NOT SEX. IF YOU FIND IT DIFFICULT, DON'T TRY TOO HARD BECAUSE YOUR PARTNER WILL BE ABLE TO TELL YOU'RE NOT REALLY ENJOYING IT. NEVER USE WORDS THAT SOUND MEDICAL – 'COCK' IS BETTER THAN 'PENIS', AND 'FUCK' IS BETTER THAN 'INTERCOURSE'.

Talking Dirty
During Sex

Loads of couples are turned on by talking dirty to one another during sex, but it's all down to confidence and imagination. Even if your partner is turned on by the idea, if you can't get past 'er, um, now put it in me… oh I feel ridiculous', you may as well forget it. You have to believe that what you're saying has the power to drive your partner wild – and it will do.

AS WITH PHONE SEX, IT WORKS BEST TO USE SHORT, DIRTY WORDS, MAKING SURE YOUR PARTNER'S HAPPY WITH YOUR DESCRIPTIONS (IT'S NO GOOD SAYING 'I WANT TO SHOVE IT IN YOUR TWAT', IF SHE'S EXPECTING TO HEAR 'I WANT TO MAKE LOVE TO YOUR HONEYED CAVE'). STICK WITH SHORT SENTENCES TOO, YOUR LOVER DOESN'T WANT TO HEAR A SHORT STORY WHEN THEY'RE CONCENTRATING ON SOMETHING MUCH MORE IMPORTANT!

If you think that your imagination is lacking, buy yourself a few erotic novels. I'm not saying that you should copy these verbatim – just get a few ideas that suit you and think about how you can adapt them.

GIVE A COMMENTARY ON WHAT YOU'RE FEELING: 'IT REALLY TURNS ME ON WHEN I TOUCH YOU HERE, IT'S SO SOFT', 'I LOVE TO HEAR YOU MOAN, I'M GONNA MAKE YOU MOAN…'. TELLING YOUR PARTNER WHAT YOU'RE GOING TO DO TO THEM NEXT CAN BE A REAL TURN-ON (BUT DON'T GO INTO LONG-WINDED DETAIL).

DON'T THINK THAT YOU HAVE TO KEEP UP A CONSTANT STREAM OF CHAT – IT CAN BE AS OCCASIONAL AS 'I REALLY WANT TO SCREW YOU,' OR 'GOD, I WANT YOU NOW...' OR ANY PHRASE THAT OUTLINES YOUR SEXUAL INTENTIONS.

Tell your lover how what they are doing is making you feel. 'That feels amazing' is a good start and you can then move on to 'you're making me really wet [or hard, or horny]', etc., which is bit naughtier.

If you get no response from your partner, simply ask, 'am I putting you off, or shall I carry on?' If they don't like it, they can just say 'It's just a bit distracting', and you'll know they're not into aural sex.

Keep your comments true and genuine, influenced directly by your feelings. As soon as you start sounding like a porn star, the whole thing's over, so don't say 'ride me, tiger, ride me with your hot tool!' unless this is the way that you both behave normally.

WHEN TALKING DIRTY, DISCUSS ANY REQUESTS OR PREFERENCES THAT YOU OR YOUR PARTNER MIGHT HAVE. FOR EXAMPLE, IF YOU WANT YOUR PARTNER TO CALL YOU 'BIG DADDY' AT THE MOMENT OF ORGASM, YOU MIGHT EXPLAIN BEFOREHAND, TO AVOID GIVING THEM A SHOCK DURING THE THROES OF PASSION.

You can also talk dirty to turn on your partner outside of the bedroom. Wait until you're in a crowded bar and whisper what you'd like to do to your lover – the naughtiness of making such a suggestion in a public place and the frustration of being unable to act on it is highly erotic. Don't make promises that you can't keep, however.

Moaning, grunting and other kinds of passionate noise-making compliment your words of lust – your lover wants to hear that they're driving you wild with excitement. No screaming though, unless you're really about to come.

It helps to have a stand-
by stock of useful 'talking
dirty' phrases. If you are
carried away with the passion
of the moment, you could all too
easily say the wrong thing, or not
think of anything to say at all.

When you become more confident with your partner, you can start to tell them what you'd like to do to them. Don't blurt out all your fantasies at once. Bring a different type of scenario into play each time. You might make it a question: "I'd love to... would you like that?" Try to sound sexy or naughty or desirable, not like you're completing a questionnaire.

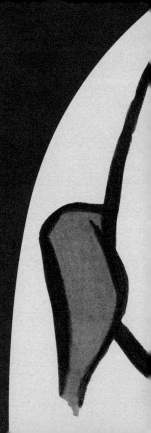

Phone Sex

The good things about phone sex are that you feel like you're being a bit naughty, which raises sexual responses, you can take pride in making your partner come by just talking to them (it's a useful skill!) and you and your partner can come together sexually when you are apart.

Don't call your partner at work for a dirty phone call unless you've had a bit of practice, you're sure that they're alone and that you are somewhere you can speak freely (though I certainly advocate the odd dirty line during a regular phone call). Use phone sex when your lover is away for the night, and call when you are both relaxed and can say and do whatever you like without being arrested.

Start gently, by telling your partner that you miss them: 'I wish you were here with me,' or 'I'm just lying in bed feeling lonely... and quite horny too'. If your partner is shy, or reluctant to join in at first, they may still be very happy to listen to you talk. Just tell them you're imagining them in your arms, and ask what they're wearing (hopefully, they'll join in and answer that they're wearing something really sexy, not just tartan pyjamas).

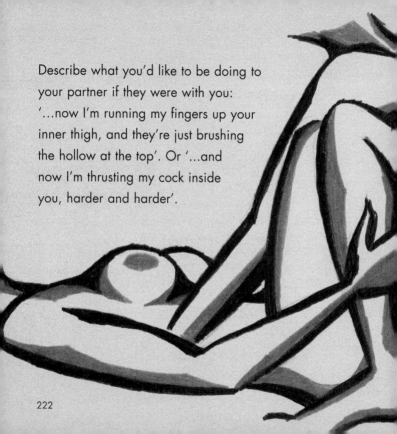

Describe what you'd like to be doing to your partner if they were with you: '...now I'm running my fingers up your inner thigh, and they're just brushing the hollow at the top'. Or '...and now I'm thrusting my cock inside you, harder and harder'.

222

Listen to the response of your lover to see if your words are turning them on. If you're unsure, ask them briefly if they want you to continue – they might just have gone quiet because they're having such an orgasmic time.

You might like to make up a fantasy story in which you and your partner are two characters. Grab your ideas from erotic novels and use your imagination when talking to your lover, telling them the location, how'd you'd both be dressed, how you would be feeling, what you'd be doing to them, etc. If you're controlling all the action, and you know you're partner well enough, you can heighten their arousal by telling them how they'd be feeling too.

If you lose your thread, don't burst out laughing and ruin the atmosphere. Go back to what you'd like to be doing and use your imagination. The more relaxed you are, the greater your imagination. Make sure that you don't just concentrate on things that will turn you on, think more of your partner and, in return, they will think about you. If you can't concentrate on turning both you and your partner on at the same time, just concentrate on your lover.

More Fun With Words

E-mailing from the privacy of your own home, to the privacy of your partner's home, can be great fun, especially if you have 'instant messenger' e-mail where your partner can immediately respond to you. Don't send dirty e-mails to work – colleagues can read them and anyone who can access the server, such as IT workers, can have a look too!

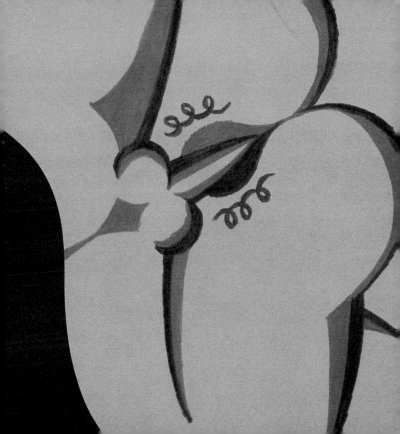

YOU CAN REALLY USE YOUR IMAGINATION ON E-MAIL BECAUSE YOU'RE NOT FACE-TO-FACE OR ON THE PHONE, SO YOU'RE LESS LIKELY TO BE SHY. PLUS, YOU HAVE MORE TIME TO THINK WHAT YOU WANT TO SAY SO YOU CAN BE A BIT MORE DARING. SET UP SCENARIOS IN WHICH YOU CAN INTRODUCE NEW EROTIC IDEAS TO YOUR PARTNER (BUT DON'T SPRING THEM ALL AT ONCE!).

Because your partner can't instantly respond to e-mail in the way that they can during a phone call, you'll lose some of the spontaneity that makes aural sex so horny. It's a bit more impersonal, too, so you might want to start with some e-mail dirty-talking and finish with a quick phone call when your need for immediate stimulation is at its height.

It can be fun to make up your own code or private meaning for certain words. This way, you can send e-mails that are as dirty and seductive as you like, without anyone knowing...

Cybersex is a whole new way of having sex. It involves fantasy, the imagination, masturbation and a PC. In online chatrooms, you can be anyone you like and say anything you want. You can imagine what you're doing to someone (or yourself) and what they're doing to you, all the time stroking yourself and masturbating. Cybersex lets you talk through your sexy fantasies with an anonymous 'partner', so that you don't have to feel inhibited or shy. This can be a very sexy experience, but if you feel unsafe or threatened in any way, then log-off immediately.

Go online to a chatroom at the same time as your partner and, assuming different names, such as 'sex kitten' and 'super stud' (plan these in advance), you can try to seduce your partner using fantasy and dirty talk. You can even do this in front of other chatroomers if you fancy a bit of online exhibitionism.

Most people have mobiles nowadays, so sending a sexy text message to your lover can be a naughty and liberating experience. It's great fun to sit on a train or bus sending erotic messages to your lover, wondering what they're doing when they receive it. It makes a boring journey so much more interesting! And when you get home, you can continue your fantasies with your partner.

'I AM HOT 4 U', 'U'R SX KTN IS GN TO WNK U', ETC.

WHETHER IT'S BY E-MAIL,
TEXT MESSAGE, ONLINE OR
IN THE BEDROOM, TALKING
DIRTY WILL MAKE YOU FEEL SEXY
AND MORE CONFIDENT AND, IF
YOU WANT TO, YOU CAN TALK ALL
DAY! YOUR PARTNER WILL LOVE IT
THAT YOU ARE SO LURVED-UP AND
IT WILL MAKE BOTH FEEL LIKE A SEX
GOD OR GODDESS.

5 POSITIONS

Missionary

The Missionary is the only position that allows you the very intimate act of kissing throughout sex, without bending down uncomfortably or bumping noses. It allows her to stroke his bum, while he has enough room to thrust deeply into her. The downside is that he can't reach her breasts, the position doesn't particularly stimulate her clitoris, and she doesn't have much room to manoeuvre. But there are variations on the Missionary position that make it a more exciting option.

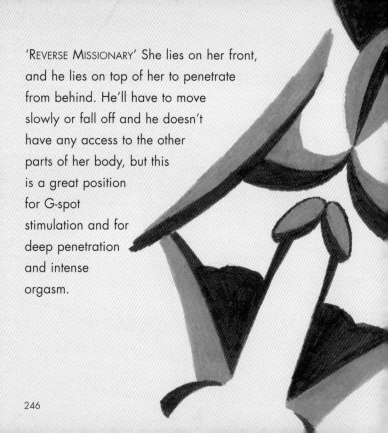

'REVERSE MISSIONARY' She lies on her front, and he lies on top of her to penetrate from behind. He'll have to move slowly or fall off and he doesn't have any access to the other parts of her body, but this is a great position for G-spot stimulation and for deep penetration and intense orgasm.

'CLOSED LEGS' This is like an ordinary Missionary position, but she closes her legs so that he's straddling her hips, creating much more friction for his penis and her clitoris. Intimate, but not much room for stroking each other elsewhere, so make this part of your routine rather than the whole.

'HALF-MISSIONARY' She lies on her back and he sits up between her legs. She puts her legs on either side of his waist or, if she's feeling particularly flexible, she can rest her legs on his shoulders. This is a fantastic position for very deep penetration and allows him to touch her breasts and clitoris as well – lucky girl!

'LEG-UP' She lies on her back (all variants of the missionary are perfect for lazy women!) and pulls up her knees so that her feet are on his chest. He gets a deep angle of penetration, she gets her G-spot thoroughly stimulated and everybody goes home happy.

'SCISSORS' He sits upright with his legs open. On her back and with her legs over his, she opens her legs as wide as she can, and holds his bum, pulling him into her with every thrust. This is a very sexy position for both partners, because you can touch each other's bodies everywhere. Movement in penetration can be difficult, however.

'BACK TO FRONT' He lies on his back this time (about time for a rest) and she lies on top of him on her back. He can caress her whole body while he's penetrating her (beware, sudden movements in this position can hurt).

'THE CURL' The woman, lying on her side, raises her upper leg. The man lies to face her and penetrates her. She can curl her leg over his body for extra comfort. There is not much room for movement, but it's a stimulating and comfortable position where neither partner has to support their weight.

Woman-on-top

Woman-on-top positions allow him the ease of access to her body that the missionary just doesn't provide. The basic format is simple – he lies on his back and she straddles him. But for red hot sex, there are variations that make it far more interesting.

Many of these positions mean that
if the woman is positioned just
above the tip of her partner's
erection, she can hold his
penis in her hand and use
it to rub her clitoris to
orgasm, then let him
penetrate her as she
comes, so he can
feel the contractions.

'GIRLS ON TOP' He lies down (good position for lazy men!) and she sits over him. He can play with her clitoris while she does the hard work of thrusting. He can further stimulate her, including stroking her breasts, and can hold onto her waist for better leverage. The position can even stimulate her clitoris if she leans forward slightly.

IF SHE LEANS BACKWARDS FROM THIS POSITION, ON TO THE BED BETWEEN HIS LEGS, HE CAN STIMULATE THE CLITORIS MORE EASILY.

'BACKWARDS' Like 'Girls On Top', but she turns around. The view of his feet isn't great, but penetration from this angle offers massive stimulation for the G-spot and he gets the chance to admire her buttocks, a visual turn-on for men, especially when they're right above his penis!

'LYING DOWN' If she lies on his chest while he's inside her, they can kiss intimately during sex, but the chance of slipping out is much higher, so she must keep her knees clamped to his sides.

'SQUAT THRUSTS' This is worth trying for the great level of stimulation it offers both of you. The vagina only has nerve endings for the first three inches and this position hits every single one of them. She straddles him in a squatting position, right above his penis. Your man can enjoy deep penetration and it leaves lots of room for wiggling around for greater arousal. For maximum arousal, lean forward and hold on to his shoulders.

If she leans backwards, elbows resting on the bed between his legs, she can maintain deep thrusting with stimulation of the clitoris.

'LEGS ROUND NECK' SHE NEEDS STRONG ARMS TO BALANCE FOR THIS. SHE SITS ON HIM, STRETCHING HER LEGS SO THAT HER FEET ARE EITHER SIDE OF HIS NECK. THIS PRODUCES EXTRA SENSITIVITY FOR HER VAGINA AND MEANS HIS PENIS CAN RUB AGAINST HER CLITORIS AND LABIA, TOO.

Doggy

Doggy positions are great for orgasm and
a big visual turn-on for him.

'BASIC DOGGY' She kneels on all fours and he kneels behind her, upright. He can penetrate easily, can hold onto her waist for thrusting and reach around to play with her breasts and clitoris too.

To increase the pressure on her G-spot in what is already a position that offers maximum depth of penetration, she can lean forwards, so her bum is high in the air and her upper body is lying down.

'EDGE-OF-BED DOGGY' She leans over the bed, resting her arms on the bed and positioning her bum at the edge of the bed. He stands behind her and penetrates her while holding her hips – an ideal position for passionate, fast sex.

IT WILL ALSO WORK IF HE KNEELS DOWN, AND PULLS HER LEGS EITHER SIDE OF HIS LAP, SO SHE'S FACE-FIRST WITH HER CALVES AGAINST HIS BACK TO PREVENT HIM SLIPPING OUT. IF HE ALSO SLIDES A HAND ROUND TO REACH HER CLITORIS, SHE CAN ENJOY A SPECTACULAR ORGASM.

TOP 5 KAMA SUTRA POSITIONS FOR THE AGILE

1 KNEE ELBOWS – STANDING UP, HER LEGS ROUND HIS WAIST, SHE RESTS HER FEET IN THE CROOK OF HIS ARM WHILE HE HOLDS HER BY THE BUTTOCKS.

2 HANDSTAND – SHE DOES A HANDSTAND, HE HOLDS HER LEGS AND PENETRATES HER.

3 CORKSCREW – SHE DOES THE SPLITS AND USES HER HANDS TO ROTATE HER BODY WHILE HE'S INSIDE HER.

4 THE CHURNING OF THE CREAM – LYING BACK, SHE PUTS HER ANKLES BEHIND HER HEAD WHILE HE KNEELS, PENETRATING DEEPLY.

5 THE TIGRESS – HE SITS, WITH LEGS SPLAYED. SHE SITS WITH ONE LEG BETWEEN HIS AND ONE LEG TO THE SIDE. WITH ONE ARM BEHIND HER AND ONE ON HIS SHOULDER, SHE LIFTS HERSELF AS HE HOLDS HER BUTTOCKS AND PENETRATES HER.

More Advanced Positions

'INVERSION' He sits on a chair or the edge of the bed, she straddles his lap, and then bends backwards so her head is almost touching the floor, while he holds onto her. The blood-rush to her head intensifies the sensations she feels, but don't do it for too long.

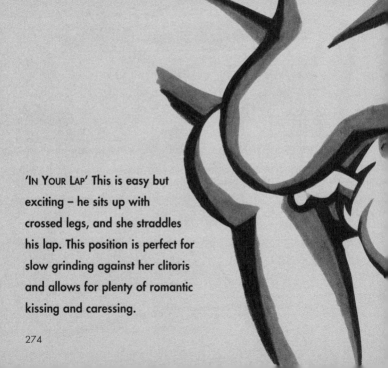

'IN YOUR LAP' This is easy but exciting – he sits up with crossed legs, and she straddles his lap. This position is perfect for slow grinding against her clitoris and allows for plenty of romantic kissing and caressing.

'OVER THE EDGE' She lies on a hard surface, perhaps a kitchen table, and he stands in front of her. The lack of flexibility in the table top means that the pressure on the genitals is intensified and leads to bigger, better orgasms (though maybe a slightly sore bum). He has access for playing and stimulating her clitoris.

'SITTING' He sits on a chair, she sits on his lap facing away from him so that he has the whole of her body to explore – he can kiss the back of her neck and reach round to play with her nipples. Gently rock to-and-fro. This is probably a position to be enjoyed for a while, before moving on to something else.

'SIDE-BY-SIDE' Sitting one in front of the other, with legs entwined – one of hers above his, or vice versa – he can thrust for a long time without coming, because penetration isn't as deep (ideal if he has a huge penis).

'STANDING UP' It helps if you're almost the same height. The woman stands against a wall and he stands in front of her. It's ideal for a quickie, and if he's strong enough, he can pick her up and wrap her legs round his hips.

ALTERNATIVELY, SHE CAN FACE THE WALL, BRACING HER ARMS AGAINST IT, WHILE HE ENTERS HER FROM BEHIND.

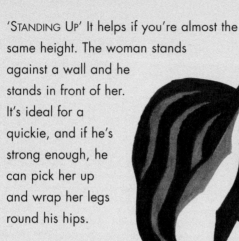

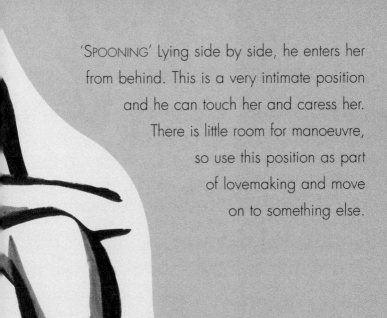

'SPOONING' Lying side by side, he enters her from behind. This is a very intimate position and he can touch her and caress her. There is little room for manoeuvre, so use this position as part of lovemaking and move on to something else.

'COITAL ALIGNMENT TECHNIQUE' (CAT) This position requires him to lie on top of her and then shift his body slightly higher than is normal. That way, his pubic bone presses on her clitoris. If he adopts a grinding, rather than thrusting, motion the chances of her coming through intercourse alone are hugely increased.

'ARMCHAIR' She lies on a large armchair, hips very near the front edge. He kneels between her open legs to penetrate her. If she likes, she can reach her clitoris to stimulate herself and movement for him is not restricted. Penetration is quite deep and can be varied by tilting her pelvis.

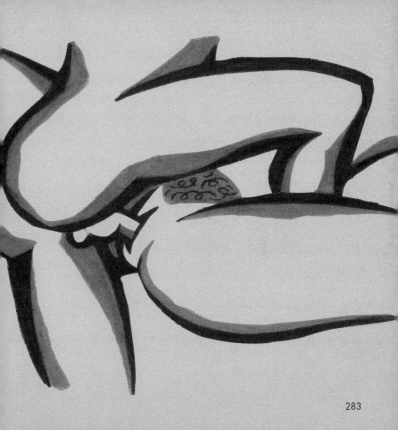

'TABLE SEX' The woman lies on a low table, feet flat on the floor. Although penetration is shallow, he can enter her from this position. If she rests her feet on his shoulders or he holds the soles of her feet while they are raised, then he can penetrate more deeply and satisfyingly.

'HEAD OVER HEELS' He lies on his back on the floor (make sure it's comfortable!) and pulls his knees up to his cheeks, ankles together but knees slightly apart. She can then ease herself onto his penis, using his buttocks for support. He can also use her back to support his feet, if necessary.

USE A VIBRATOR DURING SEX, PARTICULARLY IN POSITIONS THAT MEAN HE CAN'T REACH HER CLITORIS EASILY. SHE CAN HOLD IT HERSELF AND APPLY IT EXACTLY WHERE IT'S NEEDED.

Ladies, put a cushion under your bum to raise your hips slightly during missionary sex – this deepens the angle of penetration and allows his groin to press more effectively against your clitoris.

6 ORGASM

Orgasm should never be a goal that must be reached at all costs – too much emphasis on the end result can devalue the sexual experience altogether. It should be a leisurely stroll, not a sprint to the finishing post. But it's always nice if lovemaking can end in a shower of physical fireworks, so here's how to handle the male and female orgasm in all its guises.

Orgasm is when she's so stimulated that every nerve in her body tenses and is suddenly released in a flood of sexual sensations from the genitals.

A few women claim to orgasm just from having their breasts stroked, or even being kissed, but most will need direct genital contact to come.

Female orgasm is a delicate creature.
It requires patience, rhythm and gentleness.
Men, don't treat her clitoris like a penis.

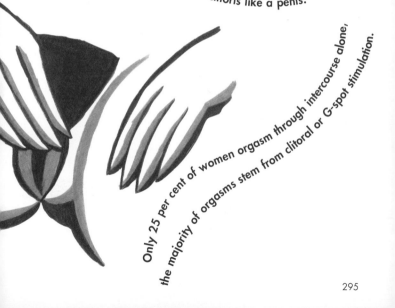

Only 25 per cent of women orgasm through intercourse alone, the majority of orgasms stem from clitoral or G-spot stimulation.

The path to orgasm often begins long before the bedroom. If a woman isn't in the right frame of mind, she can have more clitoral stimulation than a porn actress on overtime, and she still won't come. Your woman needs to be relaxed and happy with what's happening before the seed of an orgasm will even begin to germinate. If she's stressed or unsure, or feels pressurised into trying to orgasm, it almost certainly won't happen.

THE SIMPLEST PHYSICAL WAY TO GIVE A WOMAN
AN ORGASM IS BY STIMULATING HER CLITORIS –
WITH A HAND, A TONGUE, A PENIS OR A
VIBRATOR. YOU CAN SUPPLEMENT THIS
BY STROKING AND CARESSING HER
VAGINA OR BREASTS, OR
PENETRATING HER AT THE SAME
TIME. BUT IT'S THE CLITORIS
THAT HOLDS THE KEY
TO RED HOT SEX.

Orgasmic Girl – Using Your Hands

Where is the G-spot? Get on your hands and knees, and stick your bum in the air as he slips his finger inside you. This position stretches out your vagina and makes it easer to feel the little rough patch about two inches up the front wall of your vagina. Press it, adding a little extra pressure because it's hidden in the vaginal wall. When you stimulate the right spot it will swell.

Lie your woman on her back, knees raised, and sit in between her legs. From here you will have good access to the G-spot and you can play with her clitoris at the same time. She can have a fantastic climax in this position.

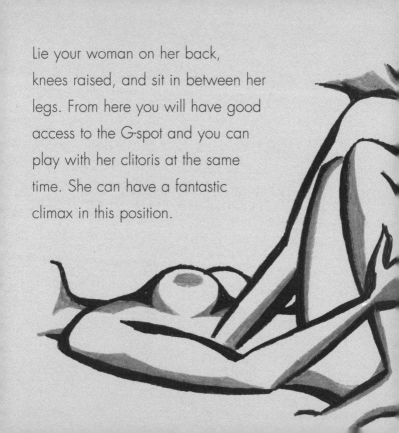

WITH YOUR LOVER LYING ON HER BACK, INSERT
TWO FINGERS AND RUB THE BOTTOM OF THE
VAGINAL OPENING, PRESSING UPWARDS
TO THE G-SPOT. THIS WAY, YOU CAN
GIVE HER TERRIFIC ORAL
SEX ON HER CLITORIS
AT THE SAME TIME
SENDING HER
SKY HIGH.

WHEN YOU STIMULATE YOUR PARTNER'S CLITORIS, THE WETTER THE BETTER. A SLIPPERY VAGINA WILL AROUSE HER MORE THAN THE SKILL OF YOUR FINGERS. MAKE SURE YOU'VE TREATED HER TO LOTS OF FOREPLAY TO GET HER WET AND BEGGING FOR ORGASM!

Use your index and middle finger, gently placed just above or on either side of her clitoris, and rub lightly in small circles. Some women prefer an up-and-down motion or more pressure as they get more turned on, but the basic move is failsafe, because it won't hurt her. Don't press too hard or too directly onto her clitoris – think of it as an expensive jewel that you're polishing delicately…

STIMULATING HER NIPPLES CAN SPEED UP HER ORGASM A GREAT DEAL – GENTLY STROKE OR LICK THEM TO AID STIMULATION BY YOUR FINGERS. BE AWARE THAT ONCE YOUR LOVER'S GETTING NEAR THAT NICE ORGASMIC SPOT, YOU HAVE TO KEEP UP THE SAME RHYTHM. ONCE SHE STARTS TO COME, DON'T RUB HARDER, JUST CONTINUE TO MASSAGE IN THE SAME WAY.

Orgasmic Girl – Using Your Tongue

First of all, be aware that you can stimulate your girl using your tongue relatively easily, but if you actually want to make her come, you've got to know what she really likes in order to get her there. You're going to have to practise lots (that's great) and listen out for her moans and sighs and be aware of the tension in her body.

Your lover is going to want lots of stimulation leading up to clitoral arousal, so don't just dive in there. Tease her all over before touching her clitoris, kissing, licking and sucking the inner and outer lips.

Men, you've really got to concentrate on the clitoris with your tongue. Yes, move away and lick and kiss other areas, roll your tongue and put it into her vagina, as far as you can go, and wiggle it around, but always come back to the clitoris.

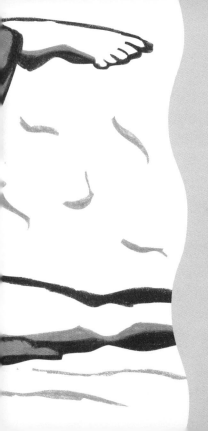

USE PROPS TO INTENSIFY
THE LICKING SENSATION –
AN ICE CUBE, A LITTLE
CREAM OR EVEN A COUGH
SWEET (CHECK OUT THOSE
MENTHOL VAPOURS).

Use your tongue to flick and lick the clitoris. Keep to the same rhythm, but don't just repeat the same manoeuvre over and over again. You might even try writing the alphabet on her clitoris with your tongue. You can use wet licks or make your tongue hard and pointy and flick, or both. When you discover the moves that she likes, don't just stick to those, remember to tease a little, only go for it when she really is at the very edge of coming.

Orgasmic Girl – Using Your Penis

The easiest way to make your partner come with your penis is not by putting it inside her and thrusting. You should use it as a glorified vibrator. Rub your erect penis along the length of her labia, so the tip is resting on her clitoris. Then just slide it up and down, slowly. The sensation is entirely different to the touch of fingers, and very sexy for both of you to feel and to watch.

You might kneel above her while she lies on her back, and hold your penis, using the tip to circle on her clitoris. It's smoother than fingers and has the added advantage that when she begins to come, you can immediately enter her. If she has a recognisable G-spot, use one of the deeper positions to stimulate it and supplement that by touching her clitoris with your fingers.

SOME WOMEN CAN COME THROUGH INTERCOURSE ALONE AND, IF SO, A FOOLPROOF TECHNIQUE IS SHALLOW THEN DEEP THRUSTING. TRY SIX SHALLOW FOLLOWED BY THREE DEEP OR, IF COUNTING SEEMS TOO CLINICAL, OCCASIONALLY PLUNGE IN DEEP, BUT MAKE SURE YOU'RE IN A POSITION THAT CAN'T HURT. YOUR LOVER WILL ORGASM FASTER IF YOU CAN GRIND YOUR PUBIC BONE INTO HER CLITORIS AT THE SAME TIME AS THRUSTING, THOUGH THAT CAN BE COMPLICATED.

321

Orgasmic Girl – Using a Vibrator

Firstly, the kind of vibrator you have affects how you use it. See the section on vibrators on page 70. As always, it depends on what your partner likes and what's really going to turn her on. And if she's not wet (and men, you should have done the groundwork here), use plenty of lube to keep things slippery!

Just because a vibrator looks like a dildo, you don't have to use it like one. Start on a 'low buzz' setting. Begin by touching it against her nipples, move it down her body to her clitoris, parting her labia slightly. Rest it alongside, rather than applying it. Move the vibrator back and forth and around, but always keep the buzzing shaft in contact with her clitoris.

To prolong arousal and intensify orgasm, remove the vibrator from the clitoris at the height of stimulation (but not when she's on the edge of coming!), then replace it. Repeat as often as she can bare it.

SOME WOMEN LIKE TO HAVE THE VIBRATOR HARD UP AGAINST THEM WHEN THEY ARE ABOUT TO COME.

Occasionally, let the tip of the vibrator touch the entrance to her vagina or, if she likes, slide it in from time to time. If the vibrations aren't intense enough, turn up the setting. If it's too intense, turn it down. If it's too intense at the lowest setting, wrap a flannel around it. Keep the vibrator moving a bit all the time – constant vibration can simply numb the nerves.

Orgasmic Boy – Making Him Come With Your Hands

When you're using your hands, don't make the mistake of swapping hands at the crucial moment because your wrist is tired . Try to keep going until he comes and rest your weary wrist afterwards.

Men need greater pressure on their penis than women do on their clitorises. Don't squeeze painfully, but a firm grip is required. Use a fast, pumping action up and down, but keep it steady. A wrenched penis is agony.

The prostate gland is the male G-spot. It is a small gland a few inches up his anus and the tip of an inserted index finger should reach it. Just stroke it gently, or rub in small circles – this is particularly effective at the moment of orgasm. You might use a small vibrator or dildo instead of a finger – these come in different sizes and will add greater intensity, depending on what your man likes. Be aware, however, that there are lots of (old fashioned) men who consider this area taboo.

USE LUBRICATION TO ADD SENSUALITY TO YOUR HAND-JOB – YOUR FINGERS WILL SLIDE OVER THE SHAFT WITHOUT DRAGGING, AND SPEED UP HIS ORGASM IF YOUR ARM'S GETTING TIRED.

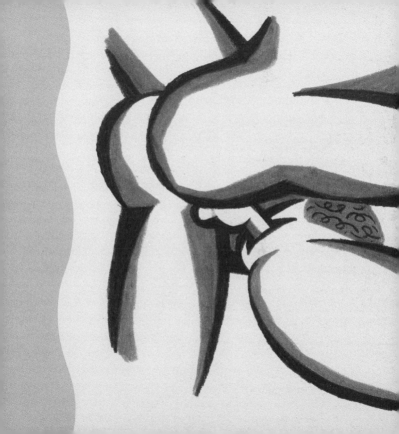

Your partner is unlikely to come without a fast, rubbing motion on his penis, so if you're unsure of what to do, ask him to show you. Most men have had plenty of masturbation practice, after all. Keep rubbing as he starts to orgasm, and continue until the last drop of semen has emerged. Unlike a woman, he generally will want you to continue rubbing while he's coming.

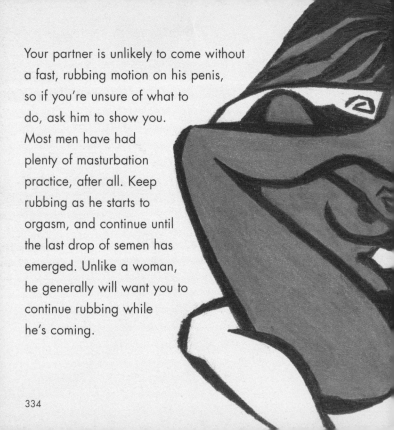

IF YOU'RE FEELING
BRAVE, STICKING A
WELL-LUBRICATED FINGER
UP HIS BUM TO STROKE
HIS PROSTATE WHILE HE
COMES WILL INTENSIFY HIS
ORGASM AND ALSO SHOOT
HIS CUM FURTHER – AN
IDEAL MOVE FOR AMATEUR
PORN STARS.

Orgasmic Boy – Using Your Tongue

IT'S MORE MOUTH THAN TONGUE THAT'S REQUIRED TO MAKE HIM COME, BECAUSE WHILE LICKING HIS PENIS WILL SEND HIM TO SEVENTH HEAVEN, HE WON'T COME WITHOUT FRICTION.

If you're serious about his orgasm, use your hand on the base of his penis and suck on as much of the head and shaft as you can fit into your mouth. Move your head back and forth, keeping your lips tightly round his penis.

WHEN HE COMES, IF YOU DON'T WANT TO
SWALLOW, DON'T LET HIM HOLD YOUR HEAD IN
POSITION. MOVE YOUR MOUTH ASIDE, AND USE
YOUR HAND TO FINISH IT OFF.

If you do swallow, keep licking very gently
when he's come – it's incredibly intimate, but
may have the power to revitalise him,
so he can penetrate you.

Orgasmic Boy – Using a Vibrator

Use the speed and power level that may be a little too much for a clitoris. Being more robust, his penis can cope with more stimulation.

AVOID PENIS-SHAPED VIBRATORS, AS THEY WILL INEVITABLY BE BIGGER THAN HE IS AND LEAVE HIM FEELING INADEQUATE. THE SMALL, SIX- OR SEVEN-INCH WAND IS MORE USEFUL FOR TURNING HIM ON.

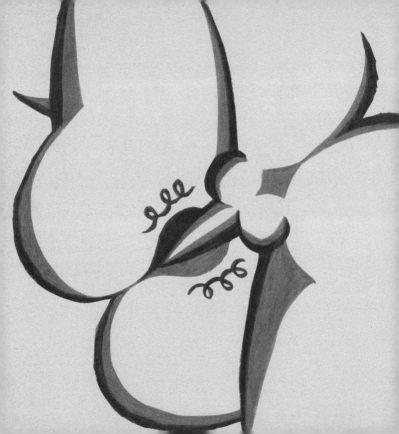

HOLD THE VIBRATOR AGAINST THE SHAFT OF HIS PENIS, WHERE THE LARGE VEIN RUNS UP IT. CLASP YOUR HAND AROUND BOTH VIBRATOR AND PENIS AT THE SAME TIME, TO INCREASE THE POWER AND STIMULATE HIS WHOLE GENITAL AREA.

Don't ignore his balls – rub the vibrator lightly across them, before pressing it against the base of his penis. This is the least sensitive area and will respond best to heavy vibration.

Hold the vibrator between you while he's inside you. This will be a big turn on during foreplay and will intensify and speed up his orgasm.

Vibrators are ideal for foreplay, creating spectacular orgasms.

Orgasmic Boy – Using Your Vagina

A VERY USEFUL TRICK TO BRING ON HIS ORGASM
DURING INTERCOURSE IS THE BANGKOK BAR GIRL
TRICK, OTHERWISE KNOWN AS CLENCHING YOUR
VAGINAL MUSCLES ROUND HIS PENIS, AS IF YOU'RE
SQUEEZING AN ORGASM OUT OF HIM.

Use the muscles you'd use to stop a wee mid-flow,
and, with practice, you'll be able to make them
clench in rapid spasms, which will feel like heaven
to him and tones you up internally too.

He needs friction to orgasm, so use a position that allows deep penetration and tightens your vagina. Doggy is perfect for this, as the angle makes him rub against the upper wall of your vagina.

For added friction, use ribbed condoms – they make look bizarre but, particularly if his penis is on the small side, they can make a big difference to how much friction you both feel.

On the whole, if he can't come, it's likely to be related to stress, tiredness or other non-sexual issues. But if the problem continues after the stress disappears, he needs to be checked physically, too.

Usually, stopping him coming is more of an issue. So try the stop–start technique. Take him to the brink of orgasm and then stop altogether until he's calmed down. Gradually keep doing this until he can hold on a little longer.

TO STOP YOUR PARTNER COMING
TOO SOON, GRASP THE AREA BETWEEN
THE HEAD AND SHAFT OF HIS PENIS
AND SQUEEZE GENTLY BUT FIRMLY
FOR A FEW SECONDS.

7 KINKY **STUFF**

For truly red hot sex, you must be open-minded. That doesn't mean that you have to do anything that you would find disgusting or might be arrested for. There are potentially loads of intense sensations that you're missing out on if you're too scared to try something new. However, don't force your partner to do anything that they don't want to do.

If you're not sure how to tell your partner about the ideas that you have, try introducing small elements of, for example, S&M, into your regular lovemaking and see how they like it. Talk about fantasies in bed and check out your partner's response. Read books together, or read your lover a 'bedtime story' that will introduce your ideas.

S&M

S&M stands for Sadism and Masochism – 'sadists' enjoy inflicting pain, and 'masochists' enjoy receiving it. The degree of pain that you can enjoy varies hugely, so you might just enjoy a very light whipping on the bum or hot wax dripped over your genitals.

ALWAYS AGREE A WORD THAT MEANS 'STOP',
SO IT'S CLEAR WHEN YOU'VE HAD ENOUGH.
DON'T USE THE WORD 'STOP' ITSELF, BECAUSE
THIS MAY BE BLURTED OUT AT A MOMENT OF
INTENSE SENSATION WHEN STOPPING IS
THE LAST THING THAT YOU WANT TO DO.

Check out our section on Toys for using bondage cuffs, whips and bats. If you want more ideas about what is available, look at specialist magazines (there should be tasteful publications around, not just hardcore) or look at sex shops online.

MEN, BECAUSE WOMEN HAVE VERY SENSITIVE BODIES, YOU'VE GOT TO GO EASY. WHAT YOU MIGHT CONSIDER PAINFUL WILL BE TWICE AS PAINFUL FOR THEM. START REALLY SOFTLY AND INCREASE THE PAIN IF SHE REQUESTS IT.

Ladies, a common scenario is to have him on all fours, blindfolded (so he can enjoy extra sensation) while you rhythmically but lightly whip his bum, increasing the pain if he wants you to. Do this for a while, then allow him to lie on his back so that you can stroke and caress him, and his penis, and tease his nipples – perhaps even putting nipple clamps on them. Then go back to whipping or stimulating him through light pain in another way.

Men, tie your lover's hands to the side of the bed so that she's kneeling, leaning forwards, with her bum in the air. Lightly, using your hand or a bat, spank her rhythmically a few times. Using your fingers or a vibrator, start to play around her genitals, maybe even inserting the vibrator into her. While you're doing this, spank her a few times, so that she is being stimulated in both places at ones. You can't carry this on for too long, because her body will get sore in this position, so untie her and caress her body for a few minutes, before starting again – maybe in a different position.

YOU BOTH MIGHT LIKE TO DRESS UP,
OR BE DRESSED UP, IN PVC OR RUBBER, A ROLE-
PLAY OUTFIT OR JUST SOMETHING BLACK AND
SEXY. DRESSING UP CAN ADD EXCITEMENT TO
ANY FANTASIES THAT YOU CHOOSE.

Anal Sex

Men tend to adore anal sex because it's dirty in both senses of the word and provides perfect friction. Women can be less keen, but this can often depend upon the size of his penis! To some, it's an odd idea, but many give it a go and they love it. However, men, you absolutely must use a condom here or you're risking very, very unpleasant infections.

Ladies, remember that you can buy a vibrator or a dildo, maybe with a harness, and you can can penetrate your man's anus. Again, some men absolutely love it and this alone, with a little genital stimulation, can make him come.

It's vital that you have plenty of lubricant, because the anus is naturally extremely dry, so use more than you think you need, and rub in on both his penis and your anus. Go to the toilet first to clear out your insides and have a good wash (it's only polite!).

THE BEST POSITION TO ADOPT IS DOGGY-STYLE. HOWEVER, IT CAN BE DONE WITH YOUR PARTNER LYING ON THEIR BACK (NEEDS A BIT OF LEVERAGE), OR STANDING UP (NEEDS HEIGHT SIMILARITIES).

The receiver must be very, very relaxed. You might try using just a lubricated finger at first, which will slide in pretty easily, then try a thin dildo. This way you can stretch the anus gradually to accommodate the larger penis. Don't 'push' anything anywhere – gently ease the penis or dildo into the anus and stop or withdraw if it hurts or becomes uncomfortable. Start again when your partner's ready.

Be aware that you can thrust in too far (it'll hurt!), so let your partner know when to stop.

Men, thrust carefully, move yourself around when you are inside her, use a vibrator or your fingers to stimulate her clitoris as you thrust – the feeling of fullness and stimulation can be a very intense turn-on for her.

Ladies, you're stimulating your man's prostate if you're giving anal sex. Alternate short strokes and long strokes as you pull your dildo in and out of him, keeping to a regular rhythm. Start slowly and speed up to a short fast pounding when he's about to come. If you can reach, touch and stroke his penis or use a vibrator. He'll go wild.

Threesomes

All the advice suggests that threesomes are a bad idea. It's true that involving another person in your sex life is fraught with danger and complex emotional issues, not least jealousy. But if you're organised and careful, then it can be tremendous fun.

Choose someone you definitely aren't going to fall in love with, such as a friend whom you've known for a while, who you can trust to be discreet. Recruiting strangers through contact magazines can feel sordid and is dangerous. With a friend, you will know each others' agendas.

BEGINNING A THREESOME IS A LITTLE AWKWARD, SO START WITH A NAUGHTY GAME (SEE PAGE 56), THAT WILL RESULT IN EVERYONE ENDING UP NAKED.

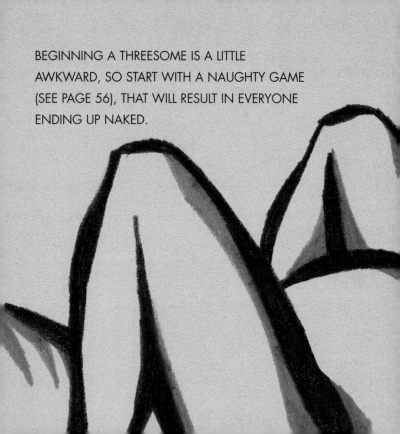

Agree any rules in advance and decide whether full sex is permitted, or only foreplay. You must take care that everyone gets equal time, unless one of you is happy to watch. If two out of the three are obviously involved with each other to the exclusion of all else, then something's gone wrong.

Whether you have two men and one women or vice versa should depend on which of you is more comfortable with the idea of having sex with your own gender.

No matter how much you enjoy a threesome don't make a habit of it, because you'll lose the exclusivity and emotional closeness of your own relationship (unless you are in a threesome relationship). You'll also risk hurting the other participant – and nobody wants to feel used.

Exhibitionism – Having Sex When You're Out And About

EXHIBITIONISTS ARE PEOPLE WHO GET THEIR SEXUAL
KICKS FROM FLAUNTING THEIR SEXUALITY IN PUBLIC.
IT CAN TAKE MANY FORMS, FROM UNDRESSING
BY A WINDOW TO HAVING FULL INTERCOURSE
IN AISLE SIX OF THE SUPERMARKET. IN MOST
PUBLIC PLACES THIS IS ILLEGAL, SO BEWARE.
HOWEVER, IT CAN BE A GREAT TURN-
ON – THE THRILL OF BEING CAUGHT
OR THE SENSATION OF THE BREEZE
ON YOUR BODY.

The naughtiest, but surprisingly common, out-of the-house sex is to pop round to your lover's office for a quickie. Rules for this are: make sure they have their own office, lock the door and draw the blinds. You might like to pop round at the end of the day, when most people have gone home, and take your chances with an unlocked door.

Ladies, surprise your man by turning up to meet him wearing a long skirt and no knickers (and don't wear a bra under that top!). You can sit on his lap in the office, or have a 'quickie' up against a wall, and the skirt will hide most of what's going on, while your lover can caress your breasts under your shirt.

MEN, IF YOU'RE EXPECTING A DATE WITH A BEAUTIFUL WOMAN IN A PUBLIC PLACE, FORGET THE UNDERWEAR AND WEAR A LONG-ISH COAT, SO THAT YOU CAN WRAP HER INSIDE YOU (AND WRAP YOURSELF INSIDE HER!) WHEREVER YOU MIGHT FIND YOURSELVES.

Ah, the great outdoors. Go for a drive in the country on a lovely warm day; take a rug, some cushions, a picnic... and lots of sex essentials! Find yourselves a secluded spot and settle down for a day of caresses, kisses and some downright dirty goings-on. You can do this on a secluded beach, but beware of that sharp, scratchy sand!

Car parks, lay-bys, vista points, alleyways, the drive outside the house – you car is a great place for a quickie. You don't have to stay in the car – if it's secluded enough, you can make the best use of park benches, picnic tables and trees (to lean against if having a stand-up quickie).

Standing up, she can put one leg round his waist for greater leverage (see page 278). She might sit up on a ledge while he stands facing her from where he can penetrate her while she wraps her legs around him. If there's room, and it won't look too obvious, you can lie down. Sitting is comfortable, and you can enjoy sex without too many glances from passers-by.

For a more hardcore thrill, it is possible – though not sensible – to have sex in a crowded club. Either she sits on his lap, having unzipped his flies, and pulls her skirt and knickers to one side, or he stands behind her and pulls her skirt up and enters her from behind. You will be noticed less if you're both surrounded by people.

You can add fantasy to your out-and-about sex. Arrange to meet your partner in a café or a bar. You have to pretend that you don't know each other – you even sit at separate tables until you start talking. You leave together and go to a cheap hotel or down an alleyway for sex. You separate and then go your different ways – maybe one goes home and the other out to meet some friends. You might arrange to meet in the back of the cinema, again pretending not to know each other.

Fantasy Sex

FANTASY IS VITAL TO GOOD SEX BECAUSE THE BRAIN IS THE MOST EROGENOUS ZONE. USING SEXUAL FANTASIES AND IMAGINARY SCENARIOS HELPS YOU TO FOCUS ON WHAT'S HAPPENING TO YOUR BODY AND OFTEN ENSURES THAT YOU ORGASM MUCH FASTER. THINKING ABOUT THE SENSATIONS IN YOUR FANTASY WILL INTENSIFY YOUR SENSATIONS IN REAL LIFE.

Use fantasies in your everyday lovemaking by taking on a role (see page 412) when having sex with your partner. Plus, of course, fantasy is great for when you are alone!

IN FANTASY, YOU IMAGINE YOURSELF IN SITUATIONS THAT WOULD NEVER HAPPEN IN REAL LIFE BUT THAT REALLY TURN YOU ON, SUCH AS BEING DOMINATED OR DOMINATING, BEING KIDNAPPED OR BEING SAT ON BY PAMELA ANDERSON.

If you're worried about your partner's reaction, introduce your fantasies to your partner very gradually, beginning by just mentioning small aspects of what you like. You should be able to gauge from their reaction whether they like the sound of it. If you want to put these into real life, then discuss that too – your lover might have some ideas of their own!

Men tend to enjoy fairly standard fantasies – recalling a memory of past sex or simply focusing on an image of sexual body parts. Men often use porn to spark fantasies, so don't be offended if you find your lover reading porn mags – he's not looking for a new girlfriend.

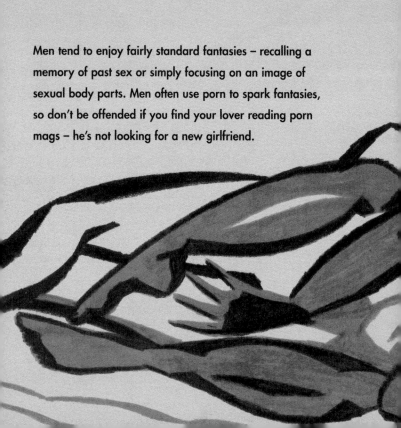

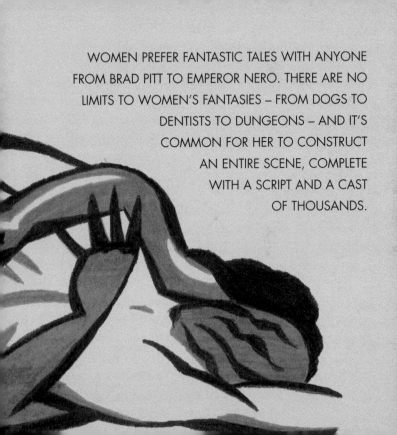

WOMEN PREFER FANTASTIC TALES WITH ANYONE FROM BRAD PITT TO EMPEROR NERO. THERE ARE NO LIMITS TO WOMEN'S FANTASIES – FROM DOGS TO DENTISTS TO DUNGEONS – AND IT'S COMMON FOR HER TO CONSTRUCT AN ENTIRE SCENE, COMPLETE WITH A SCRIPT AND A CAST OF THOUSANDS.

Common fantasy themes include sex with strangers, domination and submission, corrupting someone in authority (or being corrupted), being forced to have sex, having sex with a member of the same gender, exhibitionism and group sex. The choice is yours!

Role Play

Role play is a useful
and immensely fun way to
liven up your sex life. You
need a dressing-up box,
containing a nurses uniform,
a doctor's coat, a few bits
of school uniform, a suit
(for authority figures),
a policeman's helmet and
anything that will help to
make your personal fantasy
more convincing.

Decide beforehand what's going to happen – it will only go wrong if you assume each other knows what to do and say (unless you've done this before). If you're both imaginative enough, choose the roles and decide who is going to do what to whom, and roll with it. You might plan in advance so that you can think of ideas, phrases and scenarios to tease and turn on your partner.

TOP 5 ROLE-PLAYING FANTASIES

1 DOCTORS AND NURSES AND PATIENTS – THIS WILL REQUIRE DETAILED EXAMINATION OF BODIES.

2 TEACHER AND PUPIL – A DOMINATION FANTASY.

3 DOG OWNER AND DOG – DOWN ROVER!

4 SERGEANT MAJOR AND NEW RECRUIT – ONE OF YOU IS BOUND TO DO WHAT THE OTHER COMMANDS.

5 STRANGERS IN THE NIGHT – A STRANGER HAS PICKED YOU UP AND IS TRYING TO PERSUADE YOU TO HAVE SEX WITH THEM.

Role play can free you of inhibitions, because you're pretending to be someone else, and therefore are not subject to the usual embarrassments or worries that may stop you throwing yourself into an encounter. The sheer naughtiness of slipping out of your everyday wear (or better still, your best clothes or your work suit) and into an outfit for 'playing' can make you feel really sexy.

8 WHAT THEY **SAY**

SEX IS AN ENDLESSLY QUOTABLE SUBJECT AND THERE'S BARELY A FAMOUS PERSON ALIVE OR DEAD WHO HASN'T HAD AN OPINION ON IT AT SOME STAGE. SO IN ORDER TO MAKE SURE SEX IS REALLY RED HOT, IT'S TIME TO INVESTIGATE WHICH ADVICE IS WORTH TAKING, AND WHICH ISN'T.

A good
actress lasts and
sexual attraction
does not.

Brigitte Bardot

Brigitte is wrong – sexual attraction can last. If two people genuinely fancy each other, their desire will go through peaks and troughs, but it won't disappear – so long as you make the effort to keep it going. That means not falling into the same 'poke and twiddle' sexual routine every few nights. Make an effort to seduce each other properly, varying quickies with long, slow love-making, and always wear clean, sexy underwear, never hole-ridden pants with grey elastic.

The strongest possible pieces
of advice I would give to any
young woman are, don't screw
around, and don't smoke.

Edwina Currie

She's right about the smoking but 'screwing around', so long as you practise safe sex, can be a perfectly good way to find out your sexual likes and dislikes before you settle down with a partner. If it bothers you emotionally, of course you shouldn't do it, but sometimes you can have sensational uninhibited sex with a one-night stand. As Woody Allen said, sex without love can be an empty experience, but as empty experiences go, it's one of the best.

In love making, feigning
lovers succeed much better
than the really devoted

Ninon de Lenclos,
17th-century feminist

It's true that putting on a show of sexual passion can result in explosive orgasms all round and that once you've settled into a loved-up, cosy-couple world, the thrill of it all takes a back seat to simple, routine loving sex. But emotionally committed sex can be wild and uninhibited too. Once in a while, just going to a hotel for the night provides enough of a change to bring all the initial passion flooding back.

The age of a woman
doesn't mean a thing.
The best tunes are played
on the oldest fiddles.

Sigmund Z. Engel

After the menopause, some women find their sex drive is reduced, although HRT or its natural equivalents can help – as can a bit of lubricant. Plenty of women over 50 years old find the sudden lack of worry over getting pregnant is sexually liberating and while they may not be able to swing from the ceiling anymore, they more than make up for it in passion and experience.

[The clit is] ... Much like the stump-end of a whist-card pencil.

Dr Marian Greaves

In fact, she's wrong to describe it as the stump-end of anything. The clitoris extends beneath the folds of the labia unseen, and is actually much longer than it appears. It's a bundle of highly sensitive nerve endings, which is why her inner labia are so sensitive, and why rubbing directly onto the tip – the most sensitive part – is generally unwise.

You are throwing away the seed that
has been handed down to you as a
trust instead of keeping it and ripening
it for bringing a son to you later.

Lord Baden Powell

Obviously he was talking about masturbation and
some people still persist in believing it's bad. It isn't.
It's entirely good, in that masturbating teaches you
about your sexual need and sensitises you to all your
sensual feelings. And there is no truth in the idea that
you can 'use up' your sperm – or your orgasms – in
fact, the more you practise, the more you'll have.

A fuddled woman
is a shameful sight,
a prey to anyone
and serve her right.

Ovid

By 'fuddled' he meant drunk and while it does not serve her right, you'll very rarely have red hot sex when in a state of hopeless drunkenness – partly because to have great sex, you need some degree of co-ordination. A few glasses of wine or beer won't hurt, and may help shed your inhibitions, but men will suffer from brewer's droop after too much, and women will merely suffer from poor sex, and have more difficulty coming.

435

He twisted my nipples
as if tuning a radio.

Lisa Alther

This is one of the cardinal sex-sins. Men seldom know exactly what to do with nipples, but twiddling frantically in a bid to pick up Erotica FM is never the answer. Instead they should be caressed, lightly stroked and gently sucked. Don't pluck, tweak or twiddle.

Too much
of a good thing
can be wonderful.

Mae West

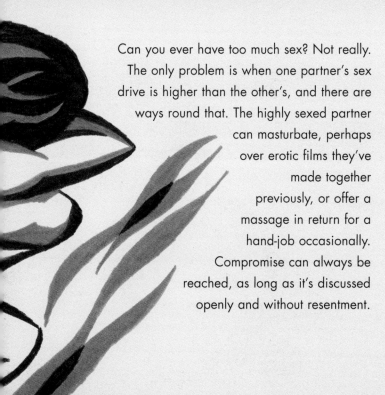

Can you ever have too much sex? Not really. The only problem is when one partner's sex drive is higher than the other's, and there are ways round that. The highly sexed partner can masturbate, perhaps over erotic films they've made together previously, or offer a massage in return for a hand-job occasionally. Compromise can always be reached, as long as it's discussed openly and without resentment.

Understandably cynical,
Marilyn was referring to the fact
that everyone is turned on by
a sniff of danger, or the thrill of
the chase. Once you're settled,
it becomes harder work to put in
the time and effort that's
required to turn your partner
on. So pretend to be strangers
and agree to meet at a
glamorous hotel bar, having pre-
booked a room. You can't discuss
anything personal. A few glasses
of champagne later, you're
having hot, unfaithful sex –
but with each other.

Husbands are
chiefly good lovers
when they are
betraying their wives.

Marilyn Monroe

Never do with your hands
what you could do better
with your mouth.

Cherry Vanilla, US groupie.

It's a myth that women always want men to
go down, and men always want a blowjob.
Sometimes a hand-job is more appealing – it's
often quicker, and it means you can kiss during
it. All the same, your mouth is a vital tool in
your sexual armoury, so don't let it go to
waste. If you suspect that your partner might
like oral sex, get right down to it and show
what you can do.

One should wear perfume
wherever one wants to be kissed.

Coco Chanel

Actually, this is a lie. For a start, perfume (or aftershave) will irritate your sensitive areas. It will also taste unpleasant, and quite possibly poison your partner. You should only wear perfume to go out. In bed, your natural, clean scent should be enough and your own pheromones are far sexier than an entire vat full of Chanel No 5.

If you want to be obscene, privacy is the most sensible option. And if you want group sex, it's wise to remain discreet. Other people's sex lives are a perennial source of fascination, and the hotter yours is, the more interesting it will be. If you are engaged in 'swinging' practices, it's vital that you trust your playmates not to blab, because you don't want to get into work and find the boss waving a Polaroid of you in the middle of a threesome, dressed in thigh-length boots.

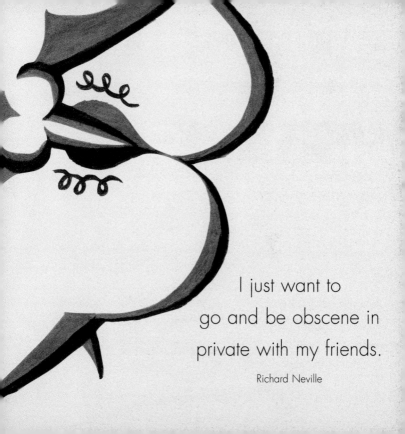

I just want to
go and be obscene in
private with my friends.

Richard Neville

One more drink,
and I'll be under the host.

Dorothy Parker

Indeed, drink does encourage a certain laxity of morals but many people believe 'in vino veritas' – or 'in wine, the truth'. So while you may be more inclined to display your more uninhibited feelings when drunk, you may be acting on desires you already have. Of course, if you're hopelessly drunk, you can't be responsible for your actions – so go easy unless you actively want to end the evening under the host, and spend the next week mailing letters of apology to everyone present.

Is sex dirty?
Only if it's done right.

Woody Allen

Finally, the neurotic New Yorker hits
the nail on the head. Red hot sex
should be dirty. It should also be
loving, fun, exciting and passionate.
And the good news is that however
experienced you are and however
old you are and whatever you look
like naked, then red hot sex can be
yours to enjoy.

The happiest part
of a man's life is
what he passes
lying awake in bed
in the morning.

Dr Johnson

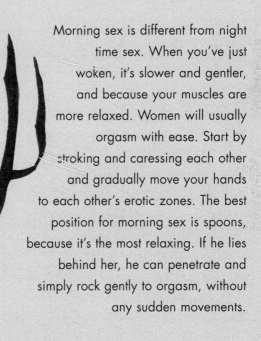

Morning sex is different from night
time sex. When you've just
woken, it's slower and gentler,
and because your muscles are
more relaxed. Women will usually
orgasm with ease. Start by
stroking and caressing each other
and gradually move your hands
to each other's erotic zones. The best
position for morning sex is spoons,
because it's the most relaxing. If he lies
behind her, he can penetrate and
simply rock gently to orgasm, without
any sudden movements.

There is hardly anyone whose sexual life,
if it were broadcast, would not fill the world
at large with surprise and horror.

W. Somerset Maugham

Perhaps the truest thing ever said about sex. Although nowadays we're much happier to discuss sex, there are certain things about your own sex life you wouldn't even tell your best friend. It's always foolish to compare yourself with others because you'll either feel inadequate – 'Why are they swinging from the ceiling when I prefer missionary?' – or else you'll feel perverted – 'Why am I the only person in the world who wants my bum licked during sex?'. There are as many sexual variations as there are couples, so go your own way, and don't worry about anybody else.

The only unnatural
sexual act is that
which you cannot
perform.

Alfred Kinsey

Nothing between consenting adults is disallowed. Whatever your background, repressed parenting or self-inflicted guilt, the truth is that as long as nobody is being forced, you can do whatever you want during sex. If she wants to call him 'Daddy' while wearing a baby's bonnet, or if he wants to pretend to be a monkey while she adopts a French accent and ties him up, then so be it. Sex is adult playtime, the only chance in a busy life that some of us get to be ourselves and share our deepest desires.

What do I know about sex?
I'm a married man.

Tom Clancy

The trouble with having something easily available night and day is that after a relatively short period of time, you can't really be bothered having it any more. At the start, relationships are nothing but passion-fuelled, rabbit-like sex then after a few months or years, sex dwindles to once a week (twice if there's nothing on TV). It's natural for sex to wane – after all, nobody could have sex indefinitely – but if it's disappearing altogether, you may wish to concentrate on improving it. This is when you need some red hot sex – new sexy underwear, a dirty weekend holiday, role play, some light bondage, the list is almost endless.

I can remember when
the air was clean and
sex was dirty.

George Burns

Of course sex should be dirty. But now it's such a talked-about topic – discussed on talk shows, in magazines and between strangers in pubs. Although openness is good, sometimes the secret nature of sex can also be fun. Breaking sexual taboos can naughty and fun. You and your lover should have your own private world in which you can be as naughty as you like without caring whether it's politically correct or socially acceptable.

If you do sleep with various partners on a regular basis, you shouldn't be made to feel guilty by anybody. The only way this is bad is if you're harming your partner or yourself by hurting them emotionally or not using protection from disease or pregnancy to protect either of you. If you sleep around because you're looking for love, as a way to build up your self-esteem, or because you don't value yourself and think casual throwaway sex is all you're worth, then you need to talk to somebody about it (ideally a professional counsellor). But if you do it because you like sex and don't want to settle down yet, then why not? If other people criticise you it may be because they're jealous – they may have fleecy pyjamas and a marital peck waiting at home, while you've got fluffy handcuffs and a night to remember.

A promiscuous person is
someone who is getting
more sex than you are.

Victor Lownes

For flavour, instant sex will never supersede the stuff you have to peel and cook.

Quentin Crisp

The longer it takes you to get to bed, the better the sex will be. This isn't always true, but there's a very good basis for arguing that the longer the seduction, the more satisfying the sex at the end of it. It is generally better if you know someone and have built up desire over a period of time – whether two weeks or two years. Anticipation is often half the fun, otherwise it's a little like reading the end of a thriller before you've finished chapter one. You may get a great orgasm with instant, first-night sex, but you won't have a great emotional connection – and the microwaved kind won't be as satisfying as the simmered-for-ages kind.

Published by MQ Publications Limited
12 The Ivories, 6–8 Northampton Street
London N1 2HY
Tel: 020 7359 2244   Fax: 020 7359 1616
email: mail@mqpublications.com

Copyright © MQ Publications Limited 2002

Text © Flic Everett 2002
Design: Philippa Jarvis
Illustrations: Alan Adler

ISBN: 1-84072-413-7

1 3 5 7 9 0 8 6 4 2

Printed and bound in Hong Kong